Metanoia and Other Sermons

Metanoia and Other Sermons

Ruskin Falls

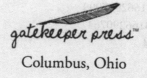

Columbus, Ohio

Metanoia and Other Sermons

Published by Gatekeeper Press
2167 Stringtown Rd, Suite 109
Columbus, OH 43123-2989
www.GatekeeperPress.com

Library of Congress Control Number: 2020952735

ISBN (hardcover): 9781662907999
ISBN (paperback): 9781662907647
eISBN: 9781662907654

Table of Contents

Prelude   vii

(1) Mark 1:14–15
Metanoia.   1

(2) Luke 9:28b–45
Even the best of disciples.   10

(3) Hebrews 13:1–6
Words to a weary church.   20

(4) John 11:17–48
Troubled and sad but not afraid.   31

(5) Mark 8:27–35
Do something brave!   46

(6) John 12:12–15, 20–25
What to hate, what to love, what to do.   58

(7) Luke 23:50–24:12
Looking for the living.   69

(8) Jeremiah 17:5–8
Desert stream.   81

(9) Romans 8:28
How the world looks to those who love God.   92

(10) Hosea 1:9b–10; 2:14–15
Our infinitely good task.   103

(11) Jeremiah 31:31–34
On the eve of destruction.   115

(12) Hebrews 1:1–3a; 4:12–13
     How the light gets in.   128

(13) 1st Peter 3:13–18a
     By gracious powers.   139

(14) 2nd Corinthians 13:11–13
     Holy kiss, triune God, and peace.   151

(15) Revelation 4:1–11
     Why worship God?   163

(16) Jeremiah 6:10, 13–15a
     The way forward.   176

(17) Matthew 19:1–6
     Whom God has joined.   188

(18) Psalm 145:1–21
     Kum ba Yah.   200

(19) Ephesians 4:17–24
     The new self.   212

(20) 1st John 4:7–16
     The love God is.   225

(21) Philippians 2:1–5
     The love we can become.   237

(22) Romans 13:8–10
     …as you love yourself.   247

(23) Revelation 1:9–2:7
     Love letters from Jesus.   259

Prelude

What follows is a collection of sermons from the weeks preceding and the first five months following our church's shift to online-only worship in March 2020 due to the pandemic outbreak of the new coronavirus, COVID-19. Each sermon is prefaced—and thereby situated in the congregation—by that Sunday's greeting and, after we went online-only, by the day's announcements. Readers outside the congregation may find the announcements, particularly the identifying of each week's worship leaders, unnecessarily repetitive. This book, however, isn't merely about the sermons. It's about how our small, electronically challenged church with its borderline Luddite minister pulled together during the first half-year of the pandemic, to keep on keeping on. This isn't just a collection of sermons. It's also a collection of services.

Pulaski Heights Presbyterian Church is a congregation small in number, most of whose members are elderly. The congregation is kind, gracious, persevering, and largely appreciative of serious sermonic wrestling with theological truth. My stated aim as preacher there is to work with sensitivity, insight, and perseverance at learning to proclaim God's word in human words that will invite understanding and renewal in the church, that will encourage among worshipers an honest, attentive, responsible, and forthright witness of faith and hope and love, and that will embolden worshipers to do God's goodness justice.

The sermons are intended as exercises in openness for the truth of God's word. Traditionalist Christians may find them doctrinally unsatisfying, not biblical enough, and less than edifying. Progressivist Christians may find them overly theological, not contemporary enough, and short on concrete social-issue engagement. In any event, a central concern throughout—a concern perhaps stated most explicitly at the end of sermon eleven—is this: the church is so like the world that it is hard for the church to hear otherworldly God's own word loving us, judging us, redeeming us, and challenging us to swim (or at the very least to paddle!) against the *many* worldly streams that, left and right, hold us back from the world that God intends. The church is ever on the verge of losing touch with—ever on the verge of needing to learn anew what it means to hear and heed—God's word. These sermons attempt to stand there on the verge and encourage Christian daring. They are neither feel-good nor finger-pointing. They are neither prosperity-promoting nor therapeutically oriented. They are not even an attempt to make the church sound relevant to the issues of the day. Rather, they simply aim at openness to the truth that sets us free for and in and through the faith and courage that Christ came bringing.

My preaching style is, I believe, more irenic than competitive in spirit. If, though, there is homiletic competition going on in what I am doing here, it is with preachers (and with myself when I number among them) who are bent *as preachers* on being conservative or evangelical or liberal or progressive or idiosyncratic or entertaining or otherwise situated *above* the word that we *as preachers* must strive to *submit to* and *serve*.

Other than that, I am not aware that I preach with an eye or ear to a particular homiletic style. I can, though, identify five books that are of particular importance to me regarding preaching: Karl Barth's *Homiletics*, Angela Dienhart Hancock's

Karl Barth's Emergency Homiletic 1932-1933, Charles L. Campbell's *The Word Before the Powers: An Ethic of Preaching*, Thomas Long's *Accompany Them with Singing: The Christian Funeral*, and Edward Farley's *Practicing Gospel: Unconventional Thoughts on the Church's Ministry*. Then, too, there is Edith Stein, who once summed it up in this way: "To stand before the face of the living God—that is our vocation."[1]

I give these sermons over to publication with a special thanks to my sister, Cherry Varee Falls, whose confidence in me so often has made up for my own lack thereof.

---

[1] Edith Stein, *The Hidden Life: Essays, Meditations, Spiritual Texts*, trans. Waltraut Stein (Washington, D.C.: ICS Publications, 1992), 1.

Mark 1:14–15 *Metanoia.*

February 16, 2020, 6th Sunday after Epiphany

Greeting
The grace of the Lord Jesus Christ be with you all!

Here, in this hour, in this place, the Holy Spirit of the resurrected Jesus Christ is at work to take what's said and sung and done here and to use all that to lift our hearts and stretch our minds toward God; to comfort us and to challenge us with God's own word; to gird us with the kind of hope and courage that nothing in and of this world, but only God, can give; and to move our wills with heavenly guidance and grace.

It belongs to my prayer that, through this service of worship, we all may experience new readiness to let our lives and our world be transformed by the gospel that Christ came bringing. Amen.

+ +

Mark 1:14–15 *Metanoia.*

Preface This is from Mark's account of what he calls *the beginning of the good news*—the beginning of the *gospel*. In these two verses, Jesus moves from a time of preparation to a time of public declaration and demonstration of his mission to the world.

1

TEXT *(English translation: NRSV)*

Now after John was arrested, Jesus came to Galilee, proclaiming the good news of God, and saying, "The time is fulfilled, and the kingdom of God has come near; repent, and believe in the good news."

(1)

For Jesus, it comes down to questions such as these: What is the greatest—what is the most profound—influence in your life? To which entities, to which things, to which powers have you most ardently entrusted the meaning and course of your life? Where do you get your basic feel for who you are and for what your life is about? What gives you the experience of being fundamentally valued? What anchors your sense of security in this world? What is the ultimate ground of hope and of courage in your life?

For Jesus, it comes down to questions such as these.

What Jesus sees is this: what we humans have turned the world into, what we have let our world become, and what we have tolerated it as is tragically at odds with and even opposed to the life that God created us to know and enjoy together. The life that you and I participate in, here in this world, actually is at cross-purposes with the life that God intends for us to be sharing together, namely, life that, left to right, right to left, top to bottom, bottom to top, and through and through, is in glad accordance with—is in joyful keeping with—and is jubilantly saturated by—the justice, righteousness, peace, and love that are the hallmarks of the kingdom of God—which kingdom still is coming to our world.

That's what Jesus sees.

And what Jesus knows is this: as long as *God* is not the greatest and most profound influence in our life; as long as it is not to *God* that we most ardently entrust the meaning and course of our life; as long as our basic feel for who we are and for what our life is about does not come from *God*; as long as we haven't experienced ourselves being fundamentally valued by and securely anchored in *God*; as long as our hope and courage are not finally grounded in *God*; then neither we nor the world around us will ever know peace; and neither we nor those around us—neither we nor our world nor our children's world nor our children's children's world—is going to blossom, bloom, grow, thrive, and flourish as wonderfully and as beautifully, as justly and as lovingly as can happen with God's help when we welcome and embrace God really, truly, genuinely, and fully as the beginning and end, as the center and foundation, of our lives and of all things.

That's what Jesus knows. And, Jesus knows that we and our world have *not*, in fact, welcomed and embraced God in this way.

Sure, we may have what's fair to call genuine faith and trust and confidence in God. And we may indeed, in many, many ways, act on and live out that faith, that trust, that confidence. And surely our gathering here in this place this morning for divine worship reflects a sense of the importance to us of looking to God as our beginning and end, the center and foundation of all things. So, it's not as if we aren't at least trying! Still, the fact of the matter is this: we have not let God's influence on our lives become as great or as profound as is the influence over us of people and things in the world around us. We have not entrusted the meaning and course of our life as ardently to God as to worldly entities, things, and powers. We have let worldly voices tell us who we are and what our life is about to a far greater extent than we have worked at hearing and heeding God's word to us. We've let not God but people and things in the world around us give us our primary lessons in what it means to feel valued. We've come to think of security solely as something we ourselves must squeeze out of the world, with little or no sense of security as something that comes from God. Likewise, whatever hope and whatever courage we have tends to be grounded in people, things, and movements within this world to the exclusion of God's word and the promise of God's coming kingdom.

And that boils down to this: our faith in God is not so great; our trust in God is not so constant; our confidence in God is not so thoroughgoing as to outweigh the power of the world around us to shape and direct our thoughts, to mold our feelings, to bend our attitudes, to goad our actions, and to steer our lives in less-than-godly ways.

You and I may think, we may feel, that we actually have done a fairly good job of welcoming and embracing God as the beginning and end of life, the center and foundation of all things. Yet, Jesus knows how prone we are to self-deception. Jesus sees through us. And he came to awaken us to what he sees. He came to admonish us not to think that we're more right with God than we really are. He came to teach us how far we and our world actually are from being the people and the world that God created us to become. He came to reveal God's holy sadness in the face of what we humans—not just some of us, but all of us together—have turned the world into, have let the world become, and have tolerated the world as, namely, a place where such things hold sway as envy and greed, jealousy and resentment, hatred and spite, callousness and indifference, false pride and false humility, arrogance and prejudice, injustice and violence, suffering and fear, the privileging of some to the detriment of others, the practice of living from a center in ourselves and in our world rather than from a center that is in God. In a word, Jesus came to awaken us to the truth of God's word to the children of Israel regarding *sin*.

In his letter to the Romans (3:10–18), the apostle Paul put that truth regarding sin this way:

> There is no one who is righteous, not even one; there is no one who has understanding, there is no one who seeks God. All have turned aside, together they have become worthless; there is no one who shows kindness, there is not even one. Their throats are opened graves; they use their tongues to deceive. The venom of vipers is under their lips. Their mouths are full of cursing and bitterness. Their feet are swift to shed blood; ruin and misery are in their paths, and the way of peace they have not known. There is no fear of God before their eyes.

If you're like me, that will sound either so harsh or so silly to your ears that you'll want to shrug it off rather than believe it. However, you can't trust Paul and you can't believe *Jesus* and not believe *that*. For that *is* the tragic truth about us and about our world that Jesus came to awaken us to—the truth about our ways of distancing ourselves from God, and so, the truth about our tendency to deceive ourselves by trying to downplay that distance in our own minds.

Jesus knows, the more comfortable we are in the world as it is, and the more at home we are in the world as it is, and the more successful we are in the world as it is, and the more content we are with the world as it is, the *harder* it becomes to see that we are caught up in a life that's at odds with God and in need of profound changes. Sure, we know we're not perfect. We know we have our faults and flaws. We know we don't always do the right thing. Still, we can't help believing that we're nice enough, decent enough, well-meaning enough, religious and God-fearing enough that surely it is an exaggeration to say that our lives and world are utterly at odds with the aims and purposes of God. And yet it belonged to Jesus's mission to awaken us to precisely that tragic truth regarding the unholy difference that exists between the life that *we* have come to enjoy and strive for and the life that *God* created us to know, enjoy, and share.

Again, you can't believe Jesus and not believe that.

(2)

Clearly, that isn't all that Jesus came to say. If it were, he would not have called it the *gospel*, the *good news*, of God. But he did. For what Jesus wants us to believe—the news, the tidings that he came bringing and that he desires for us to trust— is this: whatever you have done with your life and whatever you have made of God's good Earth, whatever distance you have let come between you and the aims and purposes of God, God is *for* you and *not against* you. God is there to be your help—your guardian, guide, and stay. Your redeemer. God is always graciously and lovingly *with* you; God is always kindly and compassionately *for* you; God is ever *with you and for you* with the help you need, to save you from whatever might put you at odds with God or steer you wide of God's good aims and purposes. God is always with you and for you, to lead you Godward. God is always with you and for you, to teach you how to take everything about yourself—even your missteps and your waywardness, even your foibles and your shortcomings, even your most grievous mistakes and your most troubling tendencies, and all your fears and sufferings—God is out to take *all that* about your past and present and to help you turn it into something good and into ways of making the world a little better, a little more beautiful, a little more wonderful, a little more kind, a little more just, a little more peace-filled, a little more godly than it was before. The gospel, the good news that Jesus came bringing, is this: God will never let you fall further from God than the reach of God's unconditional love for you, the reach of God's compassionate mercy, the reach of God's gracious determination to redeem you from anything and everything that might ever threaten to come between you and God's desire to include you in God's eternal life.

That is the gospel that Jesus proclaimed as he set out, here on Earth, on his mission of teaching, preaching, and healing in the name of God's coming kingdom.

(3)

It is in the light of that good news that Jesus begins his mission here on Earth with a call to *repentance*. And we need to distinguish between, on the one hand, *repentance*, and on the other, the *confession* of our sinfulness and sins to God. Repentance should lead to such confession. It is not, however, identical with confession. When Jesus calls us to repent, he's calling us to step out into a *change of heart* and into a *new state of mind*, in and through which we can begin to see aright the sinfulness and sins that *are* ours to confess to God.

In English, it is *repentance.* In the Greek language in which Mark wrote, the word is *metanoia. Meta* has to do with what comes after, what is beyond. *Noia* has to do with understanding, insight, thought. *Metanoia* has to do with moving *beyond* our present mindset, understanding, and attitudes, *toward* a radically new and different sense of ourselves, of our world, and of God. *Metanoia* has to do with an actually revolutionary reorientation of human life. When Jesus says, "Repent!" he's calling us to leave behind our present ways of thinking, feeling, and being in the world, in order to embrace a new and different way of thinking, feeling, and being in the world. He's calling us to acknowledge how turned away *from* God and how indifferent, resistant, and rebellious *toward* God we and our world now are; and he's calling us to acknowledge our need for profound and far-reaching changes in how we think and feel and live.

When Jesus says, "Repent!" he's calling us to ask ourselves these questions: What is the greatest and most profound influence in your life? To which entities, to which objects, to which powers have you most ardently entrusted the meaning and course of your life? Where do you get your basic feel for who you are and for what your life is about? What gives you the experience of being fundamentally valued? What anchors your sense of security in this world? What is the ultimate ground of hope and of courage in your life?

And Jesus is calling us to be honest about this tragic fact: it would be a lie or an act of self-deception to answer such questions, saying, "God is all that for me!" For the truth is this:

we have never—and, in this life, in this sinful world, we never will—really, truly, genuinely, and fully, welcome and embrace *God* as the answer to all that. In fact, we don't, on our own, even know how to *begin* doing *that*. We must be taught how to do it. And Jesus is our teacher. It is in his life and mission that we see, and it is through his word to us that we hear, what it *means* to welcome and embrace God as the answer, and what it *means* to live no longer from a center that is in ourselves or in our world but instead from a center that is in the God of the gospel that Jesus came bringing—the God who has taken gracious and loving responsibility for getting us where God knows we most deeply need to be going, the God who has always and only our truly best interests at heart, the God who always, even in all God's mystery, is at work among us, to draw forth good from all that happens, even from the presence and effects of sin and evil and suffering, thus *weaving* all that happens into God's creative aim and *fitting* us for a place and role in the future that God is calling into being, which future Jesus called God's coming kingdom.

The time is fulfilled, and the kingdom of God has come near; repent, and believe in the good news. Amen.

2

Luke 9:28b–45   Even the best of disciples.

February 23, 2020, Transfiguration of the Lord

Greeting
The grace of the Lord Jesus Christ be with you all!

Today is Transfiguration of the Lord Sunday on the worship calendar of the church. Let me begin with a few words regarding the Christian worship calendar.

In New Testament times, the church's worship calendar consisted of a year of Sundays, all pretty much alike. There were no annual celebrations such as Christmas or Easter. There was simply a year of weekly celebrations of the "Lord's Day" on Sundays. It was over the course of the church's first century that a more extensive worship calendar began to evolve.

The earliest annual commemoration was Easter, preceded by the season of Lent. Eventually Christmas and the season of Advent became annual commemorations. Then, over time, the calendar came to include such annual commemorations as Pentecost, Trinity Sunday, All Saints' Day, Reign of Christ Sunday, Epiphany of the Lord, Baptism of the Lord, and the occasion we are commemorating today, Transfiguration of the Lord Sunday.

There's good reason to let our life of worship be guided by the Christian year. This calendar's annual occasions and seasons of worship are intended to help us shape our lives and our life together around specific events in the life and mission of Jesus. The Christian calendar has evolved as a way of letting services of worship draw *our personal histories* more deeply into the *history of Jesus Christ*. These annual commemorations are designed to attune us more knowledgeably to the life of Christ, and infuse in us, over the course of time, a sounder understanding of who we are in Christ.

"The Transfiguration" refers to an experience three of Jesus's disciples had while together on a mountaintop with Jesus. There on that mountaintop, they had a vision of Jesus in which he seemed mysteriously *changed*. Matthew and Mark, writing in Greek, use the word *metamorphōo*, from which our English word *metamorphosis* derives, and which Bible translators traditionally have rendered as *transfiguration*.

The Transfiguration is the event that is depicted in the stained-glass window at the back of our church's chancel. At the bottom of the window are the three disciples: Peter, James, and John. Above them is Jesus, with two figures at his side, Moses and Elijah. Moses was famous for his prophetic role in the bringing of God's law to Israel; Elijah was famous for his role in the founding of prophecy as a religious and political movement in Israel; and, in Jesus's day, the whole of Scripture often was called "the law and the prophets." And across the top of the window are God's words to the disciples: *"This is my beloved Son, Hear ye Him."*

It belongs to my prayer today that this service of worship shall help us all more soundly and more profoundly to hear and heed Jesus, the living word of the living God. Amen.

+ +

Luke 9:28b–45 *Even the best of disciples.*

TEXT *(English translation: NRSV)*

Jesus took with him Peter and John and James, and went up on the mountain to pray. And while he was praying, the appearance of his face changed, and his clothes became dazzling white. Suddenly they saw two men, Moses and Elijah, talking to him. They appeared in glory and were speaking of his departure, which he was about to accomplish at Jerusalem. Now Peter and his companions were weighed down with sleep; but since they had stayed awake, they saw his glory and the two men who stood with him. Just as they were leaving him, Peter said to Jesus, "Master, it is good for us to be here; let us make three dwellings, one for you, one for Moses, and one for Elijah"—not knowing what he said. While he was saying this, a cloud came and overshadowed them; and they were terrified as they entered the cloud. Then from the cloud came a voice that said, "This is my Son, my Chosen; listen to him!" When the voice had spoken, Jesus was found alone. And they kept silent and in those days told no one any of the things they had seen.

On the next day, when they had come down from the mountain, a great crowd met him. Just then a man from the crowd shouted, "Teacher, I beg you to look at my son; he is my only child. Suddenly a spirit seizes him, and all at once he shrieks. It convulses him until he foams at the mouth; it mauls him and will scarcely leave him. I begged your disciples to cast it out, but they could not." Jesus answered, "You faithless and perverse generation, how much longer must I be with you and bear with you? Bring your son here." While he was coming, the demon dashed him to the ground in convulsions. But Jesus rebuked the unclean spirit, healed the boy, and gave him back to his father. And all were astounded at the greatness of God. While everyone was amazed at all that he was doing, he said to his disciples, "Let these words sink into your ears: The Son of Man is going to be betrayed into human hands." But they did not understand this saying; its meaning was concealed from them, so that they could not perceive it. And they were afraid to ask him about this saying.

(1)

We don't know just what happened that day up on that mountain. But then, Peter, John, and James themselves were not so sure what was happening, either.

It had been a long, hard trek up the mountain. The three disciples were weary. Moreover, Jesus had been praying…and praying…and praying, almost beyond their ability to keep their eyes open. Maybe you yourself have had the feeling before: you're so sleepy it hurts to stay awake, but something's going on that you know you absolutely have to stay awake for, so, with all your strength, you're fighting off falling asleep; and yet, your need for sleep is so great that it physically hurts just trying to keep your eyes open. And sometimes, in that condition, you actually can find yourself slipping into a dreamlike state, even though you're at least sort of awake.

That said, however, these disciples aren't just dreaming. Rather, they find themselves caught up, all three together at the same time, in a vision of Jesus suddenly standing before them in a new light. There's an entirely glorious flair to what they see before them. The appearance of Jesus's face is mysteriously changed, his clothes are strangely aglow, and he's conversing with two of Israel's most glorious and highly regarded prophets, Moses and Elijah. On the other hand, what they're discussing seems out of sync with the glory of the moment. For they're talking about the "departure"—and the Greek that Luke is writing in could also be translated as the "destination," or the "fate," or even the "death"—that awaits Jesus and that he is about to bring to fulfillment in Jerusalem.

The disciples have no idea what to make of what is happening.

Moses and Elijah were indeed two of the most venerated prophets in the history of Israel. They were profoundly revered for the respective roles they long ago had played in the revelation of God's word to the children of Israel and to the world. And now, precisely these so highly honored prophets, Moses and Elijah, are seen standing beside Jesus discussing the departure, or the destination, or the fate, or the death that awaits Jesus and that he is about to bring to fulfillment in Jerusalem.

You and I today, as readers of this account, know that that is a reference to Jesus's coming crucifixion. But the disciples don't know that yet, and they can't understand what all of this is all about. Peter, totally at a loss for what to say, nervously blurts out some silliness about making three dwellings there on the mountain—or, as it's sometimes translated, three tents— one for Jesus, one for Moses, and one for Elijah. What's more, something like a cloud suddenly settles over them, and the disciples are terrified. It really is Jesus who's there before them.

And yet they are scared to death. Jesus is with them. Yet they are frightened.

Then, out of the cloud, there comes a voice. Surely, it is the voice of God. And the voice declares, "This is my Son, my Chosen; listen to him." And then it's over. No more voice. No more cloud. No more peculiar light. No more flair. Also, Moses and Elijah have disappeared. The voice declares, "Listen to him," and suddenly the disciples see only Jesus standing there. They had just seen him in the company of Moses and Elijah. They had just seen him conversing with those they most intimately associated with the revelation of God's word. Then, suddenly, only Jesus is there, as if he is the one they are to listen to above all others for God's word. You might say a degree of normalcy then reestablishes itself. Except, the three disciples will not forget this experience. It will, however, take a while, before they begin to make sense of it.

(2)

I believe that New Testament scholar Douglas Hare is correct when he notes that this story of Peter, John, and James up on that mountaintop with Jesus "points us to mystery, a mystery beyond the reach of historical reconstruction or scientific verification...the mystery of Jesus' person as it was experienced by the community that grew up around him." Moreover, "the 'seeing' is not a natural function of ordinary human eyes but is God-given; God grants the disciples the power to see what otherwise would have been invisible to mortal perception."[2]

---

[2] Douglas R. A. Hare, *Matthew* (Louisville: John Knox Press, 1993), 198.

On the other hand, look closely at what happens to these disciples whom God has let see Jesus in a way no others ever had.

For starters, what they see there on that mountain confuses and frightens them. This mystical experience of Jesus does not leave the disciples feeling tranquil, serene, spiritually energized, or confident that they now are in sync with God's will. Rather, it confronts them with how poorly they have understood Jesus so far, despite their numbering among his most intimate followers. It confronts them with how short on courage they still are, with respect to trusting his cause and giving themselves over to his mission. And it confronts them with their need to acknowledge that they have yet to learn how to listen to Jesus aright and, so, how to hear and heed God's word.

Moreover, look at what happens the next day—the day following this amazing mystical experience of Jesus and of the very voice of God.

The very next day, Peter, John, and James are with the other disciples again. A man whose son is subject to being seized by convulsions comes to the disciples asking them to heal him by casting out the unclean spirit—the demonic spirit—that the father believes is the cause of the convulsions. But the disciples prove unable to do that. So, the father calls on Jesus, begging him to heal his son. Jesus rebukes the demon, heals the boy, and returns him to his father, healed and healthy again. Before doing that, however, Jesus rebukes his own disciples together with others for the faithlessness and perversity of their relationship with God. And that rebuke goes for Peter, John, and James as well, the very disciples who had been privileged to witness Jesus in what we now can call his true light—the light of his existence as the one chosen by God to reveal God's word in the world as none before him ever had. Jesus's most intimate followers, his closest disciples, even those who had been let in on that mountaintop mystical experience, don't know him as they need to know him, don't follow him as boldly as they need to follow him, don't understand his mission as they should, and, so, don't know, don't follow, and don't understand *God* as they should.

Up on the mountain, Peter, John, and James failed to understand all the talk about Jesus's upcoming "departure" in Jerusalem, all the talk about the destination, the fate, the death that awaited him there—or better, that he was going to accomplish or bring to fulfillment there in the holy city. Now, Jesus pushes the matter a step further, declaring directly to them and to the others, "Get it into your heads! Let these words sink into your ears: The Son of Man is going to be betrayed into human hands." Still, however, and all the more, the disciples fail to understand what Jesus is talking about. It makes no sense to them.

For Peter, John, and James, all the talk up on the mountain regarding Jesus's upcoming "departure" in Jerusalem did not fit with the glory and majesty of Jesus that they witnessed there. And for them and for the other disciples as well, this talk about "betrayal into human hands" didn't fit with what their eyes beheld: they had just watched Jesus drive a demon out of a person; they had just seen that his power was greater than the power of evil; they had just seen him surely looking as if he were quite in control of things and able to call the shots as he pleased; so what was he doing talking about betrayal into human hands? It just didn't fit together. It didn't compute. There was something wrong with this picture. Jesus basking in glory and majesty and rebuking demonic spirits was one thing. But all this talk of a fateful end to come in Jerusalem and of betrayal into human hands was leaving the disciples confused and making them anxious, especially after Jesus had just gotten through labeling them faithless and perverse. So, they dropped the subject.

(3)

As you and I know, things are going to get even worse for the disciples. All the way to Jerusalem, they are going to misunderstand Jesus and show themselves still faithless and perverse in relationship to him and his mission. During Jesus's final week in the holy city, these very disciples who had been so intimate a part of his mission will, in the end, betray and desert Jesus and deny to others that they even knew him. And that means this: just living close to Jesus, just traveling near to Jesus, just being around the things that Jesus said and did day to day was not enough to ready them for Jerusalem. Even that mountaintop experience of Jesus standing gloriously there with Moses and Elijah and being designated by the voice of God as God's Chosen, to whom we all are to listen, did not turn Peter, John, and James into persons with sufficient understanding and ample courage to stay true to Jesus's mission and to their calling on behalf of that mission. In the end, they betrayed, deserted, and denied Jesus and his cause. Every one of them.

If you and I get nothing else from the story of Peter, John, and James's mountaintop experience of Jesus being manifested to them in all his glory, let us at least remember this: no matter how amazingly near Jesus draws us to himself and, so, to God, we humans—even the best of the disciples—have a knack for blowing it. We have a knack for convincing ourselves that we already know Jesus better than we do. We have a knack for not really listening closely to Jesus, especially when what he has to say isn't what we ourselves are comfortable hearing. We have a knack for contenting ourselves with a faith in God that is smaller and weaker than the faith that Jesus calls for. Indeed, we have a knack for falling away and distancing ourselves from the relationship with Jesus and so with God that we actually deep down most dearly need.

In remembering all that, of course, we need to keep this, too, on our hearts and in our minds: Jesus never, ever gave up on his disciples. Indeed, even following their especially pitiful and cowardly conduct in Jerusalem when Jesus was arrested and crucified, Jesus returned to them as the resurrected one and, precisely through *them*, built up and spread the reach of his *church*. And that is what he's doing with you and me today as well. As faithless and perverse as our discipleship may sometimes be, or maybe often is, and maybe even usually tends to be, his resurrection Spirit is ever at work turning us into the building blocks of the future that God is calling into being, the future where every heart in every part of all creation shall be filled to overflowing with astonishment at and thanksgiving for the greatness of God and God's unconditionally gracious forgiveness and love.

You and I daily give God much to forgive regarding our lives and world. And daily, God responds with unconditionally gracious forgiveness and love and, too, with this command, this call, this invitation: Listen to Jesus!

Amen.

3

Hebrews 13:1–6   Words to a weary church.

March 8, 2020, 2nd Sunday in Lent

Greeting
The grace of the Lord Jesus Christ be with you all!

Today is the second of the six Sundays in the Christian season of worship known as Lent. Lent prepares us for Easter celebration of resurrection life through a period of self-critical soul-searching, meditating on the suffering and death of Jesus, pondering the nature and extent of evil around us, and doing things that help us better to heed Jesus's peculiar teaching that it is by losing yourself in the cause of the gospel that you shall find yourself, and that it is by taking up your cross that you shall truly live.

It is tempting to want to jump right over Lent and talk *only* of Easter hope and resurrection and the promise of a better time that's coming. Lent, however, keeps us mindful that the gospel isn't *only* about the *comfort and solace* that Jesus can give us. It's also about learning, through him, to look *critically* at ourselves for the *correction and redirection* we need if we are to grow ready for the future that God is calling into being and calling us to serve.

It belongs to my prayer that this Lenten service of worship shall help us all toward insight, courage, and strength in that service. Amen.

✛ ✛

Hebrews 13:1–6   *Words to a weary church.*

TEXT *(English translation: NRSV)*

Let mutual love continue. Do not neglect to show hospitality to strangers, for by doing that some have entertained angels without knowing it. Remember those who are in prison, as though you were in prison with them; those who are being tortured, as though you yourselves were being tortured. Let marriage be held in honor by all, and let the marriage bed be kept undefiled; for God will judge fornicators and adulterers. Keep your lives free from the love of money, and be content with what you have; for he has said, "I will never leave you or forsake you." So we can say with confidence, "The Lord is my helper; I will not be afraid. What can anyone do to me?"

(1)

The letter to the Hebrews isn't actually a letter. It's an early Christian *sermon*—a very long one.

We don't know who wrote it. We can, however, say this: this sermon was written for a church where membership was on the decline, enthusiasm was on the wane, and the members who had been trying to carry on as a congregation had become weary and disheartened. Despite all their hard work, their church's future wasn't looking very bright, and they didn't know what to do.

I expect that there are a lot of church folks nowadays who can appreciate theologian Thomas Long's way of describing the situation of the congregation for whom the author of Hebrews wrote this sermon:

His congregation is exhausted. They are tired—tired of
serving the world, tired of worship, tired of Christian
education, tired of being peculiar and whispered about
in society, tired of the spiritual struggle, tired of trying to keep their prayer life going, tired even of Jesus.
Their hands droop and their knees are weak (12:12),
attendance is down at church (10:25), and they are losing confidence. The threat to this congregation is not
that they are charging off in the wrong direction; they
do not have enough energy to charge off anywhere.
The threat here is that, worn down and worn out, they
will drop their end of the rope and drift away. Tired of
walking the walk, many of them are considering taking
a walk, leaving the community and falling away from
the faith.[3]

(2)

What *is* a church to do when caught in the grip of that kind
of spiritual weariness? In our own day, the tendency of such a
church is to want to find a dynamic young preacher with an
inspiring message about the benefits of faith who can come in
and rev up some exhilaration, fire up some enthusiasm, and give
the church greater emotional appeal and drawing power. Or, if
your church isn't expecting a new minister anytime soon, then
the so-called "church growth experts" might well suggest that
you talk with your old minister about maybe giving the services
of worship a peppier atmosphere that is animated perhaps by
contemporary music with a more sensual beat and more driving

rhythms than what one finds in a traditional denominational hymnal. And, too, they'll suggest that you think about new programs your church could start up that might inspire more active involvement, or that you consider new mission projects that your church would do well to get involved in that might both excite greater participation on the part of present members and attract new members as well. In any case, say the church growth experts, go to work imagining new things your church could do that would put you on the way to church revitalization, which is to say: to a surge of new life and an upsurge of fresh happenings with a renewed sense of purpose and an emotionally satisfying sense of accomplishment. And by all means, once you begin doing some or all of these things, start advertising who you are and why others would enjoy and benefit from being part of your success story.

(3)

I understand that kind of thinking. And I believe that we here at Pulaski Heights Presbyterian Church need to be asking ourselves what it means that—and what we need to be doing in light of the fact that—over the past seventy years, we've gone from over seven hundred members to under seventy members. And also in light of the fact that, over just the last few years, we've gone from a truly amazing resurgence in worship attendance to a very noticeable and perhaps disheartening decline in attendance. And note well: when we ask ourselves such questions as these, we need to keep in mind that this is not just about *our* particular church. All across the United States, small churches such as ours—and particularly those in so-called "mainline" denominations such as the Presbyterian Church (U.S.A.)—are, at an alarming rate, having to close their doors due to too few members, too little energy, and not enough money.

In light of these things, our church's session has begun setting aside time at its stated meetings for considering the situation and calling of the greater church and for considering the mission and future of Pulaski Heights Presbyterian Church in particular.

At our February meeting, for example, we took a look at recently published material from the PCUSA Theology, Formation, and Evangelism Department. The material we looked at is part of a denominational effort entitled the "Vital Congregations Revitalization Initiative." We took note of what that initiative has identified as signs of a *stagnating* congregation in contrast with what it calls seven marks of a *vital* congregation. Here are the contrasts:

1. A congregation that is satisfied with complacent "Christian" piety that simply teaches good morals and offers the latest programs is going to stagnate. The focus of a *vital* congregation will be on lifelong discipleship formation where faith strives always for deeper understanding in active engagement with the issues facing today's culture, such as injustice, inequality, divisive segregation, oppression, suffering, and abuse of creation.

2. A congregation that is satisfied with being known just for acts of charity and kindness is going to stagnate. The focus of a *vital* congregation will be on authentic evangelism, which is to say intentionally sharing the good news of Jesus Christ with others.

3. A congregation focused on institutional survival as a community of folks "just like us" is going to stagnate. A *vital* congregation will focus on growing awareness of the wider community it is part of; it will strive for closer relationship with those whose life experience may well be different from that of most current members; it will remember that Christ dwells among the lowly and the least, with the stranger and the foreigner, with those marginalized as minorities, as well as with those whose life experience has been that of society's majority.

4. A congregation that looks solely to the pastor for leadership is going to stagnate. A *vital* congregation, on the other hand, will identify, nurture, and support the use of the spiritual gifts of all people to serve in shaping and charting their congregational course.

5. A congregation where worship is about self-gratification, stale ritual divorced of meaning, or consumer entertainment, is going to stagnate. In a *vital* congregation, worship is about letting the Holy Spirit open up a clearing around us where God's own word can make itself heard, challenging, teaching, transforming, and convicting us, and sending us out into the world as somehow different than we were when we came in.

6. A congregation that acts like one social club among others, satisfied with half-hearted programmatic participation, lukewarm faith, and a lot of pretending, is going to stagnate. A *vital* congregation is about caring relationships shaped by God's true agape, where, girded by mutual love, people confront conflict, seek reconciliation in the face of divisions, find ways of

embracing diversity, and seek to be peacemakers and bridge-builders together.

7. A congregation where finances are not transparent, where generous giving is not encouraged, where money is not responsibly budgeted, where it's unclear who is making decisions, where obsolete and irrelevant buildings become more important than the work they were intended to house, and where the pastor and other staff aren't given adequate time off from work is going to stagnate. In a *vital* congregation, all are aware of how decisions are made; the views and insights of all are valued and taken seriously; church finances are handled responsibly and transparently; the work of the church is held in higher regard than the building that houses it; and there is a supportive attitude regarding the health of the pastor and other staff.

(4)

While the session has begun this conversation, the task of distinguishing between stagnating and vital congregations, and the work of keeping us on the path of the latter and not letting us turn into the former, is not the job of the session alone. It's up to all of us over the weeks and months ahead to become a part of that conversation and activity. And I look forward to where this process takes us!

That is, though, all I'm going to say about that this morning. For what I want to do now is this: I want to point out what the author of Hebrews offers to the disheartened few who, even as their congregation has grown oh-so small and poor and weary, nevertheless have remained loyal to the mission of the church and gone on striving on behalf of its cause. What the author of Hebrews offers to the weary few is this: an extremely long *sermon* that holds up before them *three important reminders* regarding what constitutes the *true vitality of the church*.

The first reminder is this: God is in heaven; we are on Earth; and there is no natural bridge from here to there. Left to ourselves, we have no way of getting to God, no way even of knowing whether or not God is. And if God is, we have no way of knowing who God is, what God's attitude toward us is, or what God is up to with us in the end. Left to ourselves, we're left without true knowledge of God. However, God has acted to *reveal* to us God's reality, truth, and presence. God has acted to lift us up into God's own life and thereby into true knowledge of God. God has done this by coming among us in Jesus Christ and, through his life and mission, speaking into our hearts and minds the love that is who God is, the love that is God's attitude toward us, the love that is what God is up to with us in this life—and beyond.

The second reminder is this: we know all this because, through the *church's* proclamation of the gospel of Jesus, his Holy Spirit opens up in and among us the eyes and ears of Christian faith. And through this gift of faith, the Holy Spirit goes on to enable the church to be how and where God's word reveals itself in the world and so, how and where God's word is to be heard and made effective in the world.

The third reminder is this: as *hearers* of God's word, we are to be *doers* of God's word. And that means we are to look to Jesus as the one through whom and through whom alone we know God truly, the one whose guidance we are to follow even when that means swimming against the stream of raging worldly waters, and even when it means cutting against the grain of powerfully entrenched worldly attitudes and ways.

Those three reminders add up to this: the church is God's way of blessing us to become hearers and proclaimers of God's word; the church is God's way of turning us, God's way of converting us, into doers of God's word; and conversion happens as we are challenged to let Jesus shape our hearts and minds and actions. The church, therefore, is how and where people learn to embrace that *blessing* and take up that *challenge*.

That is what Hebrews offers to Christians who are disheartened regarding their congregational future, who are weary with how things are going, and who are uncertain what to do next! It's not exactly a perky pep-talk about the worldly benefits of participating in the church. It's more a stark imperative to church members, declaring, *Have no fear! Don't let yourselves be defined by worldly ideas of success! Just let the church be how and where, through congregational witness to the life and mission of Jesus, God's word is proclaimed and heard—then let God's word be done in your life! And then, humbly yet boldly, boldly yet humbly, leave the rest to God!* And note well: not only is Hebrews less a perky pep-talk than a stark imperative, but in chapter thirteen, from which this morning's passage comes, the sermon actually closes with examples not of how following Jesus will make us feel good about ourselves, but of how *challenging* it is, truly to follow Jesus. In today's reading, we can hear five examples of how challenging it is.

First example: to follow Jesus is to follow the path of *mutual love*. And note well, the Greek word translated here as "mutual love" is φιλαδελφία (*philadelphia*), literally, "brotherly love." We don't follow Jesus by giving ourselves over to some vague and general "love of humankind." We follow Jesus by loving others the way one should expect to love and be loved by *family*. Following Jesus is about loving others not simply as our fellow human beings somewhere out there in the world, but loving them as family should love, which is to say, as those whose joys, concerns, tragedies, and well-being are intimately entwined with our own.

Second example: to follow Jesus is to practice *hospitality to strangers*. It's not simply about enjoying the company of folks like ourselves or folks we otherwise know and like. It's about looking to people we've never met and to people who may seem different from ourselves, maybe even *disconcertingly* different, and seeing, precisely in those people, persons we need to serve in ways that make them feel at home.

Third example: to follow Jesus is to go where life is shaped by *empathy* toward others in their times of trial and suffering. Where Jesus is, the trials and sufferings of others are met, not with callousness or indifference, but also not just with sympathy, pity, or feeling sorry for them. Rather, *their* trials and sufferings are met with *our* concerned participation *in* those trials and sufferings. When we follow Jesus, we let the trials and sufferings of others become a source of trial and suffering of our own. We may pity, but we don't *simply* pity, those in prison. We may feel sorry for, but we don't *just* feel sorry for, those being tortured. Rather, we let concern for their eventual well-being so penetrate our own soul that *we* experience *their* trials and sufferings with a familiarity and intimacy that lets *us* feel *their* pain and actually *participate* in *their* agony.

Fourth example: to follow Jesus is to learn to let *desire* be turned from lust and greed into joy and freedom. It means refusing to reduce sex to the selfish use of another person, but, instead, to let sex involve delight and exhilaration before the *mystery* of that person's being. It means to let sex involve a personal commitment to the other's integrity and good. And, to follow Jesus means to refuse to let money and possessions become essential to our sense of fulfillment and meaning; it means to refuse to pursue them as things we're madly driven to accumulate; it means to let our life become so rooted in trust in the goodness and faithfulness of God that we become freed *from* the power of money and possessions and free *for* enjoying them as things we gladly, graciously, and generously share with others.

Fifth example: to follow Jesus is to *let our life be steered* not by voices out to conform us to the world as it is, nor by voices out to conform us to their own self-serving agendas and schemes, but, rather, by openness to the *God* of Jesus Christ; the God whose thoughts and ways are radically different from the thoughts and ways that the world is out to surround us with and inculcate in us; the God who speaks into our hearts and minds the wisdom and courage to say "No" to any and every voice that speaks contrary to God's world-changing and life-transforming word.

Let it be said one time more this second Sunday in Lent: the sermon we call Hebrews is not exactly a perky pep-talk about how much worldly gratification and success people's participation in the church will add to their life. It's more a stark imperative to church members, in which we hear declared, *Have no fear! Don't let yourselves be defined by worldly ideas of success! Just let the church be how and where, through congregational witness to the life and mission of Jesus, God's word is proclaimed and heard. Then let God's word be done in your life! And then, humbly yet boldly, boldly yet humbly, leave the rest to God!* Amen.

(4)

John 11:17–48

Troubled and sad but not afraid.

March 15, 2020, 3rd Sunday in Lent

Greeting
The grace of the Lord Jesus Christ be with you all!

On the Christian calendar, today is the third Sunday in Lent, the period of forty regular days plus six Sundays preceding Easter. Lent is intended by the church as preparation for Easter celebration of resurrection life through a period of self-critical soul-searching, meditating on the suffering and death of Jesus, giving prayerful consideration to the extent of evil and suffering around us, honestly pondering our own mortality, and doing things that help us better to heed Jesus's peculiar teaching that it is by taking up your cross and losing yourself in the cause of the gospel that you shall find yourself and truly live.

I realize that the question of the meaning of Lent is not what looms largest in people's thoughts today, but, rather, the question of what to do in the face of the present pandemic outbreak of COVID-19.

There are seven types of human coronavirus. First identified in the mid-1960s, four of them are very common and cause only a mild illness. More recently, there have been outbreaks of two other coronaviruses that have been more serious. They are the SARS coronavirus that caused an outbreak in 2003 and the MERS coronavirus that caused an outbreak in 2012. And now this novel—or new—coronavirus, whose outbreak began in December 2019.

We have included in today's bulletin an insert regarding COVID-19 from our government's Centers for Disease Control and Prevention (the CDC). There's much, much more information on the CDC website. If you haven't already, I encourage you to check it out.

Many churches have canceled worship services for today and some even for the next month or more. And many that *are* open have taken such measures as canceling baptisms and the sharing of the Lord's Supper until further notice.

It is possible that today could turn out to be the last day *we* will hold Sunday services for a while. At our stated meeting following worship today, the session will be discussing what our church needs to do moving forward. For today, the session chose to hold this service of worship, though with a few wise adjustments to how we go about it.

For starters, not only is there plenty of soap and water in the restrooms, but we also have lots of hand sanitizer readily available.

Moreover, according to the CDC, the new coronavirus is not, like a flu virus, airborne—it doesn't hang around in the air, waiting for you to breathe it in. Rather, it's thought to be spread by respiratory droplets from another person, droplets that fall to the ground rather than floating in air, droplets that you can protect yourself from by keeping a distance of six feet between yourself and an infected person.

So, we're inviting everyone to stay spread out today for safe measure. And when it's time to pass the peace of Christ, rather than walking up to each other and shaking hands, we ask that you remain where you are and pass the peace to others with a respectful bow or gracious wave of the hand.

We know that the new coronavirus has poor survivability on surfaces it falls onto. It can't live, for example, on our offering plates. Still, preferring to err on the side of caution, rather than everyone passing the plates hand-to-hand, we're going to ask the ushers to keep the plates in their hands and go around to everyone.

As health agencies have emphasized, this is not a time to let fear and panic rule our lives. Cooler heads need to prevail. But a cool head is one that is reasonably cautious. We all need, in this anxious time, to stay constantly and reasonably cautious. To be sure, most folks who have gotten the virus have not needed hospitalization—just a few weeks of home rest. In some cases, one is barely slowed down at all. For some, though, particularly the elderly and those with compromised immune systems or with chronic conditions such as heart or lung disease or diabetes, hospitalization is absolutely called for. Especially among the likes of these, this disease can have fatal results. In any case, COVID-19 is going to work an enormous stress on the entire U.S. health-care system. It's also having a drastic impact on many people's income and livelihood and on such considerations as schooling, childcare, and also eldercare.

The CDC expects that, before it's over, most of the U.S. population will have been exposed to this virus. In the U.S., as of yesterday, there were more than twenty-seven hundred confirmed or presumptive cases. The illnesses have ranged from very mild to severe, and there have been more than fifty deaths. And those figures can be expected very, very rapidly to rise much, much higher.

Socially, politically, economically, medically, the situation in the U.S. right now looks menacing and even dire. In my sermon today, however, I'm not going to have anything more to say about that. I have no great in-depth analysis or social/political commentary or words of wisdom to add to all the other voices I'm sure you've been hearing this past week. Rather, my goal has been simply this: to take the passage of scripture that has impressed itself on me as needing to be preached today, listen to it as best I can for what the gospel of Jesus has to say to us here, let you know what I think I heard, and then leave it to the Holy Spirit to use *my* words to guide *you* to what God wants *you* to hear today.

I *will* note that the text this morning is the story of Jesus's raising of Lazarus from death, and I *will* be talking about our attitude toward death. And, yes, I do expect that COVID-19 is going to cause many more deaths in the weeks and months to come. Also, however, today *is* the *third Sunday in Lent*. And, traditionally, Lent *has been*, among other things, a time for letting each of us have this hard fact impressed upon us: *We are dust, and to dust we shall return.*

It belongs to my prayer that, on this Lord's Day in this strange time in this, in so many ways, so prosperous land, each person here shall hear and feel the presence with us of the God of our salvation, the Lord of healing, the shepherd who truly supplies our needs. Amen.

+ +

John 11:17–48   *Troubled and sad, but not afraid.*

Preface In the course of his mission, Jesus's reputation has been growing—both his reputation for troubling the religious and political authorities and his reputation for dazzling folks with wonders. When Lazarus, whom Jesus deeply loves, falls critically ill, his sisters, Mary and Martha, send for Jesus to come to the village of Bethany where they and their brother live. Before Jesus's arrival, however, Lazarus dies, and his body is placed into a tomb.

TEXT *(English translation: NRSV)*

When Jesus arrived, he found that Lazarus had already been in the tomb four days. Now Bethany was near Jerusalem, some two miles away, and many of the Jews had come to Martha and Mary to console them about their brother. When Martha heard that Jesus was coming, she went and met him, while Mary stayed at home. Martha said to Jesus, "Lord, if you had been here, my brother would not have died. But even now I know that God will give you whatever you ask of him." Jesus said to her, "Your brother will rise again." Martha said to him, "I know that he will rise again in the resurrection on the last day." Jesus said to her, "I am the resurrection and the life. Those who believe in me, even though they die, will live, and everyone who lives and believes in me will never die. Do you believe this?" She said to him, "Yes, Lord, I believe that you are the Messiah, the Son of God, the one coming into the world." When she had said this, she went back and called her sister Mary, and told her privately, "The

Teacher is here and is calling for you." And when she heard it, she got up quickly and went to him. Now Jesus had not yet come to the village, but was still at the place where Martha had met him. The Jews who were with her in the house, consoling her, saw Mary get up quickly and go out. They followed her because they thought that she was going to the tomb to weep there. When Mary came where Jesus was and saw him, she knelt at his feet and said to him, "Lord, if you had been here, my brother would not have died."

When Jesus saw her weeping, and the Jews who came with her also weeping, he was greatly disturbed in spirit and deeply moved. He said, "Where have you laid him?" They said to him, "Lord, come and see." Jesus began to weep. So the Jews said, "See how he loved him!" But some of them said, "Could not he who opened the eyes of the blind man have kept this man from dying?" Then Jesus, again greatly disturbed, came to the tomb. It was a cave, and a stone was lying against it. Jesus said, "Take away the stone." Martha, the sister of the dead man, said to him, "Lord, already there is a stench because he has been dead four days." Jesus said to her, "Did I not tell you that if you believed, you would see the glory of God?" So they took away the stone. And Jesus looked upward and said, "Father, I thank you for having heard me. I knew that you always hear me, but I have said this for the sake of the crowd standing here, so that they may believe that you sent me." When he had said this, he cried with a loud voice, "Lazarus, come out!" The dead man came out, his hands and feet bound with strips of cloth, and his face wrapped in a cloth. Jesus said to them, "Unbind him, and let him go."

Many of the Jews therefore, who had come with Mary and had seen what Jesus did, believed in him. But some of them went to the Pharisees and told them what he had done. So the chief priests and the Pharisees called a meeting of the council, and said, "What are we to do? This man is performing many signs. If we let him go on like this, everyone will believe in him, and the Romans will come and destroy both our holy place and our nation."

(1)

By the time Jesus set out for Bethany, his life already was under threat from many directions. Some viewed him as a reckless disturber of the peace; some saw him as a trickster, some as an insult to the honor of God, and some as an offense to social decency and propriety. Some even wanted him dead. In particular, the religious leaders and governing authorities wanted to be rid of him.

A little background in that regard. Several decades earlier, the Jewish people had been conquered by and made subject to the military rule of a pagan government—the Roman Empire. The Jews were allowed to keep some of their own local governing authorities, but only so long as those authorities served the aims of Roman law and order—the so-called Roman peace. Jerusalem was the seat of Jewish governance, and in Jerusalem were some of Jesus's most powerful detractors. Jesus knew that he would not be safe in or near Jerusalem.

The town of Bethany *is* near Jerusalem. Nevertheless, Jesus's presence and help are needed there, and so, he goes to Bethany, the hometown of Mary, Martha, and Lazarus. Lazarus is dead when Jesus arrives. Jesus prays to God, then calls on the once-dead Lazarus to come out from the tomb. Still wrapped in burial cloths, Lazarus comes out and rejoins the living.

This raising of Lazarus gets two reactions from people there. Some see it as a sign that it is *God* who is working through Jesus. They believe in him as the bringer of help and salvation from God. Others see it as the work of a rabble-rouser out to wow the masses into joining his movement; he is, they say, encouraging disrespect for the law; he is, they say, clearly *not* a friend of Caesar; he is, they say, up to things that are going to cause Rome to ban every vestige of Jewish self-government that they have left. Those who know that Jesus is stirring things up that could bring Rome's wrath down hard on the Jewish people become set on finding a way to stop him. Better that he should *die*, they say, than that he be allowed to cause Rome to lower its military boom with full force on the entire Jewish people.

Jesus is aware of increasingly violent opposition to his mission. This shows in what he does when, in the passage following the one we just read, he departs from Bethany. Leaving Bethany, Jesus at first hides out close by, near a wilderness area, for some peace and quiet. However, the time for the Passover festival is at hand, and Jesus wants to celebrate this Passover with his disciples. That means spending a week in Jerusalem. So, Jesus comes out of hiding to go to the Holy City, even though he knows that the powers-that-be will not appreciate his presence there. And they don't. At week's end, Jewish authorities will arrest Jesus, and Roman authorities will execute him. By the end of the week, Jesus will be dead and his body placed into a tomb.

(2)

As the apostle Paul emphatically reminded his fellow Christians in the church in Rome, Christian baptism involves *baptism into Christ's death* (Romans 6:3). More broadly, of course, Christian baptism is baptism into Christ's *life of grace.* In that life, there is such nearness to God's love and mercy and forgiveness that we can sense that we never need fear being condemned or abandoned by God, and we can sense that we've been set free to say yes to Jesus, even as he calls to us on the way to his *crucifixion,* saying, "Come, follow me." You and I have been set free by Christ to *challenge,* with unheard-of *courage,* all powers and forces in this world that stand in the way of God's good aims and purposes among us. This is a courage that is ready to risk suffering and even *death* in Christ's cause, convinced that, as Paul put it, *If God is for us, who can be against us?* (Romans 8:31).

Sometimes, for some Christians, the call to follow Jesus does indeed become a call that leads steeply into the valley of the shadow of death—a call that demands *readiness to die* for one's witness to Christ in service to God's coming kingdom. Maybe we're not all called constantly to witness to Jesus in ways that incur mortal risk. Nevertheless, throughout history, and in times, places, and certain circumstances still today, the path of Christian discipleship has been paved with challenge, danger, agony, and death.

An example that I was reminded of recently is that of the Dominican nun, Dorothy Stang. She was in her mid-seventies when her death was reported fifteen years ago, in February

2005. Originally from Ohio (and with a sister here in Little Rock), she found herself called by Jesus to serve among the poor who live in the jungles of the Amazon rainforest. In service to the gospel of Jesus, she lived with and worked on behalf of the poor in that region for many years. She participated in guarding the well-being of their villages. She also defended their rights against powerful groups, powerful outside interests, that were set on employing stealth to take away the villagers' land and mine its resources for themselves. And she stood up for the villagers there, despite the death threats she sometimes received from such groups. In February 2005, she was assassinated by two gunmen apparently hired by land speculators whose get-rich plans were being obstructed by this nun and her now-growing village. Witnesses said that, as the assassins approached her, she calmly opened her Bible and began to read, ready to die for rather than abandon what she had felt called by Christ to do, with and for the people there. Such readiness means *casting yourself completely on the grace and love of God to be your courage*. And that's what she did. And it is what Christ calls all of us to be prepared to do.

Of course, that doesn't mean it shouldn't matter to us whether we live or die. Rather, it means that it is given to us to have unheard-of *courage* in the *face* of death. It means that it is given to us, so to *trust* the gospel of Jesus, that the *fear* of death can't hold us back from the things that Jesus is calling and giving us to do.

Still, that doesn't mean that death ceases to sadden and disturb us. After all, death saddened and disturbed even Jesus. That's what we're told in the story of Jesus and Lazarus. In the company of those who were mourning Lazarus's death, Jesus himself was, we read, so greatly disturbed and so deeply moved that he began to weep. In the wake of the death of Lazarus, Jesus wept.

(3)

Some people claim that if Jesus really was the Son of God, if Jesus really was the word of God become flesh, then death shouldn't have had the power to affect him in this way. Death shouldn't have shaken him. What I hear in this passage, however, is a tender description of Jesus's genuinely human nature. I hear confirmation of the church's longstanding affirmation of faith, that God was uniquely present in Jesus's person, revealing God's glory through him without displacing anything about him that was truly human. Jesus was personally so unimaginably *intimate with God* that God's own will, God's own way, God's own word, revealed itself through him without his ceasing to be genuinely human. And it just is genuinely human not to want to die; it is genuinely human not to want our loved ones to die; it is genuinely human to find God's gift of life so good, so sweet, so beautiful, and so precious that it becomes one's deep, deep, deep desire to be allowed to enjoy this life forever. It is genuinely human to be saddened, even tearful, when confronted with death's reality, particularly the death of a loved one or the inevitability of one's own death.

Death has an uncanny power to anguish and to grieve us humans. It is, for us, disconcerting that, while it is certain that we are going to die and disappear from this Earth, we don't yet know just what happens *when* we disappear. We know we're *going* to disappear, yet we don't *understand*—we can't *comprehend*— that disappearance. We can see the dust to which death one day shall return us, but we cannot see beyond that dust. Death confronts us as a *power of darkness* that is the *enemy* of all that is light and beautiful and precious and good about life.

In the face of death, Jesus, too, was filled with human uncertainties. For him, too, death was a power of darkness that is the enemy of things light and beautiful and precious and good. And when, for example, his friend Lazarus died, Jesus hurt; he even cried. Still, Jesus also had a supremely intimate trust in God to lift us humans beyond death's darkness and into God's eternal life. Jesus even had a supremely intimate confidence in God's use of Jesus's own life and mission to *reveal* to people the *reality* of resurrection life. That doesn't mean that Jesus was in a position to say just what form, ultimately, resurrection life is going to take for us. But it does mean that he didn't fear death, and it means he wants *us* not to fear death any longer. He wants us so to trust God's desire and power to give new life, that, though death may *trouble* us and make us *sad*, it emphatically will *not* be allowed to make us *afraid*.

(4)

That, I believe, is where the story of the raising of Lazarus is pointing.

The event is filled with urgency and sadness. There is a sense that there is something so precious and wonderful and beautiful and good about being alive here on God's wondrous Earth, that the destruction of life, the loss of life, *naturally* can only cause us sadness and tears. However, the raising of Lazarus is not intended finally to *save* anyone from sadness or from death. After all, Lazarus *is* going to die again. And whether it be in a few days or only after several years, this time he won't be rejoining the living here on Earth. Rather, he will disappear, and his loved ones will be reduced to sadness and tears. The point of what Jesus did was not to save Lazarus from death, nor to save his loved ones from their sadness. The point, rather, was this: *to let the death of this dear friend be turned into the revelation of God's glory as the one who gives new life beyond the grave.* Jesus's raising of Lazarus is not to say death shouldn't sadden us. It's to say *we need not be afraid.* For, looking to Jesus, we can be constantly ready and courageously joyful, even when brought face-to-face with the reality of death—even the death of a loved one, and even when we sense our own impending death.

A powerful reminder of what it means to be constantly ready and courageously joyful even when death is looming before us or over us comes in the closing lines of the sermon Martin Luther King, Jr., delivered the evening before his assassination in 1968. On that evening, he declared the following from the pulpit of a local church:

> Well, I don't know what will happen now. We've got some difficult days ahead. But it doesn't matter to me now. Because I've been to the mountaintop. And I don't mind. Like anybody, I would like to live a long life. Longevity has its place. But I'm not concerned about that now. I just want to do God's will. And He's allowed me to go up to the mountain. And I've looked over. And I've seen the promised land. I may not get there with you. But I want you to know tonight, that we, as a people will get to the promised land. And I'm happy, tonight. I'm not worried about anything. I'm not

fearing any man. Mine eyes have seen the glory of the coming of the Lord.[4]

That sermon, in all the tragedy we now know was hovering over that hour, is a good example of the kind of *joy* that Jesus calls us to. It is not at all a superficial joy. It is not a joy obtained by ignoring all the sadness that haunts human life. It is not a joy obtained by forgetting, evading, not talking about, or refusing to confront, the fact that we are going to die. Rather, it is a joy that involves remembering each day that *this day might be my last.* It is a joy that's fully aware that every step we take might be our final step. It is a joy that has learned to be open and honest about our mortality, open and honest about our own approaching death, so that we may cast ourselves completely on the grace and love of God to give us *courage*—the grace and love of the God whose desire and power it is to raise us up into new life.

(5)

Today is the third Sunday in the Christian worship season known as Lent. Much of what the season of Lent is about is precisely God's gift *of* and our need *for* Christian *courage* in the face of suffering and death.

The first day of the season of Lent is known as Ash Wednesday, which fell on February 26 this year. The day is commemorated in some churches with an Ash Wednesday service of worship. The point of such a service includes helping us begin our Lenten journey to Easter by taking to heart these

---

[4] James M. Washington, ed., *The Essential Writings and Speeches of Martin Luther King, Jr.* (San Francisco: HarperCollins, 1986), 286.

things: that we *are* mortals; that the way to Easter resurrection *is* through death; and that, rather than living in fear of death, we should live humbly yet boldly turned toward *Jesus,* grateful for the good news that he came proclaiming and demonstrating, that he might breathe divine courage into these oh-so human lives of ours.

Central to an Ash Wednesday service is the imposition of a cross of ashes on the forehead of each worshiper. And each time that cross of ashes is marked on someone's forehead, the words are spoken: *"Remember that you are dust, and to dust you shall return."*

Those ashes and these words are a reminder to us of the frailty and uncertainty of human life, and of our need for a courage that, no matter what and come what may, can gladly, gratefully, and serenely declare: *I'm happy, tonight. I'm not worried about anything. I'm not fearing any man. Mine eyes have seen the glory of the coming of the Lord.*

It belongs to my prayer that each of us may learn so gladly, gratefully, and serenely to trust God's power to give life that, though death may make us *sad*, it nevertheless won't be allowed to make us *afraid*, and though death may strike us as an enemy, it nevertheless won't be allowed to steal from us the peace and joy and blessing that eternal God desires for all God's children to know and share—here and now, and forever. Amen.

Mark 8:27–35   Do something brave!

March 29, 2020, 5ᵗʰ Sunday in Lent

Greeting
The grace of the Lord Jesus Christ be with you all!

On the worship calendar of the church, today is the fifth Sunday in Lent. Lent is a season of worship intended by the church to help us prepare for Easter by engaging in times of prayer and in other activities that ready us to appreciate this truth: that the God of Easter resurrection is the God who comes to us through the Jesus Christ who *suffered and died* so that we might know—and so that we ourselves might embrace—God's passionate and compassionate love for the world and God's desire and expectation that we now strive to see and challenge the workings of sin and evil in the world in the *light* of the *cross* of *Jesus*.

During Lent we are called, among other things, to examine, question, and deepen our *commitment* to Christian discipleship by taking seriously and taking to heart the peculiar Christian claim that true life is the life that calls to us from the *cross of Jesus Christ*; that following Jesus has to do with *denying ourselves* and *taking up our own cross*; and that it is by *losing ourselves* in the work of the gospel that we shall *find ourselves*.

In this morning's sermon, I will be taking up important aspects of this peculiar Christian claim. Before getting to that,

46

however, I'd like to offer a word regarding the reason why we're not worshiping today in our sanctuary but, instead, on the World Wide Web. We're doing this because of the health and safety measures the public has been asked to observe due to the new coronavirus and the disease it causes, COVID-19.

On March 11, the World Health Organization characterized the outbreak of COVID-19 as a pandemic. The following day, the CDC (the Centers for Disease Control and Prevention) suggested that before it's over, most of the U.S. population will have been exposed.

As you know, most folks who have gotten the virus have not needed hospitalization—just some home rest. In some cases, one is barely slowed down at all. For some, though, particularly among the elderly and those with compromised immune systems or with chronic medical conditions, hospitalization can become vital and the hospital care intensive. Especially for persons in these latter groups, the disease can have fatal results.

No one knows just what course COVID-19 is going to take, or how bad it will or won't get, or for how long or how short a time it will keep us in crisis mode. It does, though, seem fair to say that it got a head start on us. While the disease is racing forward, we're playing catch-up both on testing supplies and on the hospital beds and equipment and personnel we're being told we need. And neither a cure nor a vaccine is to be expected soon. And it's not only our personal health and our health-care system that are taking a hit but also our incomes and our livelihoods. More and more and more people are being laid off from their jobs, and more and more existing businesses are being faced financially with having to close their doors. And all this, right now, is happening with no clear end in sight though the government *is* now poised to step in, as, without this help, many millions will be driven into sheer desperation. And even *with* government help, *if* the disease spreads as rapidly and as widely as *could* happen, the financial ill effects on individuals and communities, and the forced rationing of health-care resources among the afflicted, could spell a crisis unlike anything most of us are prepared yet to imagine. And this, not to mention the long-term effects that social isolation and the minimizing and distancing of face-to-face encounters are going to have on us all, as individuals and as a society.

Socially, politically, economically, medically, the situation in the U.S. right now is looking menacing. In my sermon today, however, I'm not going to say anything specifically about that. I have no great in-depth analysis or social/political commentary or words of wisdom to add to all the other voices I'm sure you've been reading and listening to this past week. Rather, my goal for today is simply this: to take the passage of scripture that impressed itself on me as needing to be listened to on this fifth Sunday in Lent, to listen to the text as best I can for what the gospel of Jesus has to say to us here, to let *you* know what I *think* I heard, and then to leave it to the Holy Spirit to use *my* words to guide *you* to what *God* wants you to hear today.

It continues to be my prayer that, on this Lord's Day in this strange time, in this, in *so* many ways, so prosperous land, we all shall hear and feel the presence with us of the God of our salvation—the Lord of healing—who can and will meet us in our deepest needs, to comfort, challenge, and direct us, like nothing in and of this world, in redeeming ways. Amen.

+ +

Announcements

In the event that someone's watching who's not a member here or who is not otherwise a regular or occasional attendee:

My name is Ruskin Falls. I serve as minister for Pulaski Heights Presbyterian Church. Though we're housed in a large building, we're a small, mostly older rather than younger, and *not* technologically savvy, congregation. And I myself do have a reputation for being unduly dismissive regarding "social media" and people's fascination with photos and videos of themselves. Today, though, I admit that I am grateful to have this wonderful technology and some folks who know more than I do about making it work so that we can all join together in at least this semblance of corporate worship.

This is our first try at doing this. And that is a reason why we're actually recording it on a Thursday afternoon to make available to you on Sunday morning. For now, going the prerecorded route seemed more workable to us than what is called live-streaming. We'll see how it goes. And please feel free to share with me any suggestions you have for how we might do it better next week and beyond.

I hope, in the weeks ahead, we can include more of the things that we usually do in worship that we're not going to try doing today. For this, our first fledgling effort, we're going to go with a very modest order of worship: a reading of scripture, a sermon, some piano music, and a prayer.

We're not even going to make time for passing around a virtual offering plate! However, I do want to remind our members that, if, in this time of financial distress, you are able to keep your giving to the church up to date, then please keep it on your heart and in your mind to do that. Members—indeed *anyone* who would like to contribute to the work of this church—can send contributions by mail to our church office, or you can donate by using the PayPal option on our website. The PayPal option is at the bottom of our homepage. Let's all do what we can as we can in this difficult time.

+ +

Mark 8:27–35   *Do something brave!*

Preface The Gospel of Mark was written in Greek. The Greek term, ὁ Χριστός, *the Christ,* means what the Hebrew term we translate as *the Messiah* means, namely, "the anointed one." Both terms identify the one chosen by God to manifest God's saving presence in the world. Thus, ὁ Χριστός can be translated either as *the Christ* or as *the Messiah.*

TEXT *(English translation: NRSV)*

> Jesus went on with his disciples to the villages of Caesarea Philippi; and on the way he asked his disciples, "Who do people say that I am?" And they answered him, "John the Baptist; and others, Elijah; and still others, one of the prophets." He asked them, "But who do you say that I am?" Peter answered him, "You are the Messiah." And he sternly ordered them not to tell anyone about him. Then he began to teach them that the Son of Man must undergo great suffering, and be rejected by the elders, the chief priests, and the scribes, and be killed, and after three days rise again. He said all this quite openly.

And Peter took him aside and began to rebuke him. But turning and looking at his disciples, he rebuked Peter and said, "Get behind me, Satan! For you are setting your mind not on divine things but on human things."

He called the crowd with his disciples, and said to them, "If any want to become my followers, let them deny themselves and take up their cross and follow me. For those who want to save their life will lose it, and those who lose their life for my sake, and for the sake of the gospel, will save it."

(1)

Ours is a world laden with sin; ours is a world haunted by ungodly powers: powers of hatred and mistrust, jealousy and resentment, arrogance and prejudice, greed and injustice, oppression and persecution, sickness and suffering, complacency and indifference, chaos and death. Peter expected the coming of the Christ to mean the coming of the kingdom of God that would spell the end of these ungodly powers. He wasn't ready for a Christ who would suffer and die at the hands of such powers.

What about us? Are we ready to believe that God, creator of the heavens and the earth, has acted to reveal God's reality, truth, and saving presence, not by ending worldly opposition to God's coming kingdom, but, rather, through a Messiah, a Christ, who was tortured and killed on a cross? Are we ready to believe that God has spoken to us decisively through someone who sat imprisoned on death row; who, in his final agony, was beaten, stripped naked, held up to public ridicule, and then tortured and killed by crucifixion?

You and I do have the advantage of having read the end of the book. Although Christ suffered and died, God raised him up from death. He's our crucified *but now resurrected* Lord. So, in that sense, we don't have the problem that Peter had that day on the way to Caesarea Philippi.

But there's more: in raising Jesus from the dead, God wasn't just demonstrating God's power over death. The resurrection was not simply God's act of overturning how Jesus died. It was God's act of vindicating how Jesus *lived*. It was God's act of justifying Jesus's *cause*. It was God at work declaring that the graciously compassionate justice, peace, love, and mercy that the disciples had heard Jesus proclaim and had watched him live out are indeed the hallmarks of God's own coming kingdom. The resurrection was God at work revealing to Peter and the other disciples back then, and to you and me today, that the life and mission of Jesus, that the words and deeds of Jesus, are our window to the future that God intends for the world, and God's way of declaring what is ours to do for the sake of that future. The resurrection is God at work revealing, for example, that we are to hear God's own word coming at us when Jesus declares on the way to his cross, "If any want to become my followers, let them deny themselves and take up their cross and follow me."

(2)

What does Jesus mean by *deny yourself*?

For starters, he means what he said to Peter: stop setting your mind on human things and not on divine things. "Your tendency," says Jesus, "is to think about God on the basis of *human* thoughts about God. Your tendency is to begin with hopes and desires that you think you need divine help in fulfilling—or to begin with fears you have of things a divine being *might* do—and then to think of God in those terms. However," Jesus goes on, "you've got to stop thinking about yourself first, and only afterward about God. You've got to stop thinking human thoughts first and only then thinking about God. You've got to stop doing all your thinking from a center that is in yourself and learn instead to think from a center that is in God."

But how do you do *that*?

For starters, in order to think from a center that is in God, you have to stop thinking that you can teach yourself God's reality, truth, and presence, and you must instead let *God* do the teaching. You have to let *God* teach *you* who God is and what God's attitude toward you is and what God is up to in your life. To think from a center that is in God, you have to stop thinking about God on the basis of what you either hope or fear that God is like; you have to stop thinking about God on the basis of what you assume God *must* be like in order to *be* God. And, instead of all that, you have to let *God* teach *you* what to think of God. And precisely *that* is what God has done and does for us in Jesus Christ! In the life and mission of Jesus, we meet with very God declaring to us who God is, what God's attitude toward us is, and what God is up to with us. Setting our minds on divine things—thinking from a center that is in God—means learning God's reality, truth, and presence—learning God's word and will and way—not by looking first to ourselves, but by first learning Jesus Christ. We don't meet with God by turning toward our own thoughts and feelings. We meet with God by looking to the life and mission of the crucified but resurrected Jesus Christ and learning to follow him.

(3)

And there's the rub: cross-bearing, self-sacrifice, is not what we by nature want our life to be about. The very thought makes us feel the way Peter felt that day on the way to Caesarea Philippi: *it makes us want to rebuke Jesus!* It makes us think, "Surely there's a better way! After all, doesn't our faith in God seem already fitting enough without our becoming involved in things like cross-bearing and self-sacrifice?"

Think, too, about this: Jesus was known—and was complained about by some of his opponents—for his *festiveness*. Their complaints suggest that our picture of Jesus is incomplete until we can picture Jesus *smiling*! Our picture of Jesus is incomplete until we can envision him enjoying a hearty feast with a goatskin of wine in the company of very earthy individuals who are laughing, dancing, and enjoying life's goodness. Our picture of Jesus is distorted if we picture him as somehow untouched by Earth's beauty and delights or if we think of him as not wanting *us* to be touched by them as well. Jesus knows that God intends for life on Earth to be enjoyed.

And, yet, there is something not right about the way that we have come to enjoy the world. There's something not right about the way that we have come to enjoy…ourselves. If life is to be saved, there is something about us that must die. Peter, that day on the way to Caesarea Philippi, thought he knew a better way. "Get away from me, Satan," said Jesus.

(4)

What is it about us that must die?

That will vary from person to person. No two of us are just alike. We have different strengths and different weaknesses;

different temptations and different capacities for resolve; different talents and different ways both of using and of squandering those talents; different fears and differing ways of dealing with them; and differing personal, social, and political inclinations. Christ's call to each individual is particular to that individual. It's particular to us as the individuals that we respectively are. The cross that Christ is calling *you* to take up will be uniquely yours.

It is important to note, however, that Jesus is not talking about cross-bearing the way we often do when we refer to some hardship we happen to be undergoing as "my cross to bear." Jesus is not talking about just any hardship, burden, loss, or pain that we might now be having to hold up under. And he isn't talking about something we can't decide to walk away from. To the contrary, Jesus is talking about a cross that we must *choose* to take up and that we also can *choose* to put down. For what Jesus is talking about is this: *the cross of discipleship*.

What Jesus is saying to Peter and, so, to us, is that the call to discipleship comes with a *warning*. The warning is this: you live in, and your life is entwined with, a world of *sin*. Sin is the fact that our world constantly chases after false gods while shunning the will and way of the one true God. Sin is the fact that our world is in the grip of, and is constantly inculcating in us, such traits as jealousy, envy, and resentment; arrogance, hubris, and prejudice; callousness and indifference; rancor and spite; inequity and injustice; chaos and violence; deception, self-deception, and lies. Sin hinders and disengages our ability to embrace the graciously compassionate justice, peace, love, and mercy that are the hallmarks of the life and mission of Jesus. If, therefore, you choose to answer the call to discipleship—if you say yes to the call to begin letting Jesus teach you who God is, who you are, and what God desires for your life to be about—don't expect the world to make it easy for you. Rather, expect to find yourself called to swim against the stream of many common assumptions, popular opinions, and personal tendencies. For sin has led us all to enjoy ourselves in ways—it has led us to divide the world up in ways, and to guard our personal privileges in ways, and to cling to goods and possessions in ways, and to judge ourselves and others in ways—that run counter to the life that Jesus calls us to embrace and share. A yes to Jesus, therefore, will at least sometimes entail self-sacrifice. Following Jesus can be counted on repeatedly to alert us to something in us that has to die. In order to live in keeping with Jesus's life and mission, there always will be some tendency in us, some inclination, some wont, some habit of thought, some desire, some need, some security blanket, some worldly attachment, some dream, some hope, some longing, some fear that has to die—that has to be let go of, put aside, overcome, and moved beyond.

The question, therefore, is this: how do we discover what it is in us that has to die? And my suggestion is this: keep always in mind that, in this world that crucified Jesus, discipleship is as much about *courage* as it is about *faith*. In a sinful world, you can't say yes to Jesus and never have to cut against the grain of what's popular, what's normal, what's comfortable, what's easy, what's inviting, and what feels safe, secure, and reassuring. It isn't Christ you're listening to, if you never hear him calling you to do things that take *courage*. And it's precisely when you do sense Christ calling you to do something that calls for courage, and maybe more courage than you think you presently have, that you learn what it is in you, what it is about you, that you must let go of, put aside, overcome, and move beyond, in order to follow Christ. For what needs to die is whatever in you resists serving Christ's graciously compassionate justice, peace, love, and mercy.

In this respect, we can be helped by a line that the sixteenth-century Protestant reformer Huldrich Zwingli was famous for using to tell people how to follow Jesus. He declared simply, "For God's sake, do something brave!"—not as a matter of reckless endangerment; not as a matter of bluster or bravado; not as a matter of gallantry or heroism; not for the sake of proving anything at all to anyone at all, but simply for God's sake, for the sake of letting Christ's graciously compassionate justice, peace, love, and mercy shine more brightly in our world: *Do something brave.* Do something that is a yes to Jesus Christ, even though it means cutting against the grain and swimming against the stream of what's popular, what's normal, what's comfortable, what's easy, what's inviting, and what feels safe, secure, and reassuring. For the sake of what Christ has taught you about the future that God intends, *do something brave!* Amen.

(6)

John 12:12–15, 20–25

What to hate, what to love, what to do.

April 5, 2020, Passion Sunday

Greeting
The grace of the Lord Jesus Christ be with you all!

This is the sixth and final Sunday in the season of worship the church calls Lent. Today the church commemorates the day when Jesus arrived in Jerusalem with his disciples to prepare for the Passover Feast. The gospels note that, as Jesus entered the city, people hailed him with shouts of "Hosanna!—Save us, we beseech you! Blessed is the one who comes in the name of the Lord!"

The gospel of Luke tells us the people spread out cloaks on the road in front of Jesus. The gospels of Matthew and Mark add that they also spread out leafy branches. The gospel of John notes that they were waving branches from palm trees. When today is referred to as Palm Sunday, it's those palms in the gospel of John that are in mind.

In light of the COVID-19 pandemic that we're in, some may be finding it hard to get into a "Palm Sunday" state of mind. When I say "Palm Sunday" state of mind, I'm thinking of the popular image of Jesus's entry into Jerusalem as a festive parade lined with happy faces, cheerful hearts, and waving hands, all

58

riding on the spiritual high they've been given by Jesus, as he himself rides triumphantly into town. And that's not where most of us are today. Right now, we aren't feeling so triumphant. We're not riding that kind of spiritual high. We're not up for a parade. Instead, we're looking at family and friends being distanced from each other, sometimes quarantined, maybe even getting sick, or maybe dying; we're looking at a health-care system that may be getting catastrophically overloaded and health-care workers and public servants being pressed far beyond the usual call of duty; we're looking at an economy that, at an alarming rate, has been closing down businesses, knocking people out of incomes and livelihoods, and wrecking hopes and dreams; we're looking at public institutions all operating in crisis mode. Things are feeling too dark for a parade.

But think about what Jesus surely knew. He wasn't parading into the limelight; he was riding into the heart of darkness. He could see coming the darkness of the week ahead: it would be painful and bitter; it would be filled with controversy; there would be attacks aimed at him; and there would be the threat of torture, humiliation, and death. Indeed, the church has come to refer to what actually happened to Jesus that final week in Jerusalem as *the Passion of the Christ*, the English word "passion" deriving from the Latin word "passio," which means "suffering." That is why this day also is referred to in the church as *Passion Sunday*. Today marks the beginning of the week of *the Passion of the Christ*, the week of his ride into the heart of darkness.

It belongs to my prayer that we'll be drawn this day to sense both Christ's passion and his compassion, and drawn as well, whatever happens and come what may, to stand with him,

knowing that, whatever happens and come what may, he stands
with us. Amen.

✛ ✛

Announcements

For the sake of any visitors we have today, let me identify myself.
I'm Ruskin Falls, and I serve as minister here at Pulaski Heights
Presbyterian Church. Due to the health and safety measures
that the public has been asked to observe because of COVID-
19, we're not meeting face-to-face in our sanctuary. Rather, I'm
here on a Friday afternoon with three other members of our
church: our liturgist, LaWanda Harris; our pianist, Sally Todd;
and our church sexton—who's now also in charge of this video
effort we've just begun—David Harper. And we're recording
something we hope can draw our church family worshipfully
together, even at a distance, this Sunday morning. And before
going further, let me let the three of *them* wave hello to you.
Sally, if you could step over this direction. And LaWanda. And
David, if you'd step around yourself to wave hello. Thank y'all.

Last Sunday was our first try at offering worship in this way.
My thanks to those who, over the course of the week, suggested
ways to improve on the start we made last week. We know that
the audio wasn't as strong as it needed to be, and some of you
had difficulty hearing me. I believe, and at least hope, we solved
that problem this week. But remember, we're still learning how
to do this, so we still welcome your suggestions for ways to do
it better.

As we did last week, so also this week, we're abbreviating
the order of worship that we usually follow here on Sunday

mornings, but this time, only a little. LaWanda has joined me today, and we're going to include more of the things we usually do together on a Sunday morning. I hope that what we do here will serve to give us all a worshipful sense of belonging together this day and belonging to God.

+ +

John 12:12–15, 20–25 *What to hate, what to love, what to do.*

TEXT *(English translation: NRSV)*

The next day the great crowd that had come to the festival heard that Jesus was coming to Jerusalem. So they took branches of palm trees and went out to meet him, shouting, "Hosanna! Blessed is the one who comes in the name of the Lord—the King of Israel!" Jesus found a young donkey and sat on it; as it is written: "Do not be afraid, daughter of Zion. Look, your king is coming, sitting on a donkey's colt!"

Now among those who went up to worship at the festival were some Greeks. They came to Philip, who was from Bethsaida in Galilee, and said to him, "Sir, we wish to see Jesus." Philip went and told Andrew; then Andrew and Philip went and told Jesus. Jesus answered them, "The hour has come for the Son of Man to be glorified. Very truly, I tell you, unless a grain of wheat falls into the earth and dies, it remains just a single grain; but if it dies, it bears much fruit. Those who love their life lose it, and those who hate their life in this world will keep it for eternal life."

(1)

Jesus is arriving in Jerusalem. The city is filled to overflowing with Jewish pilgrims who've come to celebrate the Passover. Passover is a commemoration of the time when God, through the leadership of Moses, delivered the Israelites from slavery in Egypt, so that they might live free in a homeland of God's own choosing. There, God would turn them into a light to the nations. They would become a people through whom all the families of the Earth one day would learn God's graciously loving and liberating reality, truth, and presence.

Right now, however, the children of Israel are not free. They are subjects of the Roman Empire. They are under the military rule of Caesar and his minions, including the Roman governor for the region around Jerusalem, Pontius Pilate. A few days ago, Pilate made an awesome entrance into the city to remind all Passover pilgrims that they are subject to Roman authority and power. He came astride a mighty horse; he came with a display of imperial pomp; he came at the head of an intimidating procession of armed cavalry and foot soldiers; he came flaunting banners proclaiming the person, power, and peace of Caesar—Caesar, who has come to be addressed throughout the empire with such titles as "Son of God," "Lord," and "Savior."

Today, Jesus is entering the city from the Mount of Olives. I'm told that it is customary for Passover pilgrims to walk into the city. Imperial rulers and Roman cavalry ride in on their mighty steeds. But everyone else walks into Jerusalem at Passover. The fact that Jesus comes in riding means he's up to something. And, seeing Jesus contrast himself to the Romans on their mighty steeds by riding in on a lowly donkey, people realize he's making a political statement: He's making light of, he's lampooning, the arrogance of imperial power. And, as Jesus enters the city gates on his little donkey, some of his more daring followers do their part, shouting, "Hosanna!" which means "Save us, we beseech you!" "Hosanna!" they shout. "Blessed is the one who comes in the name of the Lord, the King of Israel!"

What is taking place there in the streets of Jerusalem is high-drama street theater. Politically powerless Jesus and the political nobodies who have become his followers are spoofing and calling into question and even challenging how Caesar and his minions wield political power. Excitement, suspense, and tension fill the air. Hearts are in the grip of exhilaration. It is a powerful and, for the disciples, empowering moment. As Jesus enters Jerusalem on a donkey, they begin to hail not Caesar's representative, but Jesus as the one to whom they intend to be loyal. It is a jubilant moment. Revolutionary spirits are high.

What, though, is the first thing we hear Jesus talk about after he arrives? He talks about death. One moment, followers are cheering him into the Holy City with jubilant words, "Blessed be our Lord and King. Save us, we beseech you!"; the next moment, Jesus quiets them with talk about...dying. He starts by noting that a grain of wheat has to die in order to bear fruit. And I can imagine people thinking, "Well, yeah, sure. What about it?" Then Jesus says, "If you love your life, you lose it, and if you hate your life in this world, you'll keep it for eternal life. Stop loving your life! Learn, instead, to hate your life!"

(2)

Jesus's words stop our jubilation cold. What in the world could he mean?

I invite you today to take that question up by considering how I believe it was taken up by Christians in the early decades following Jesus's crucifixion and resurrection.

We're talking about a time when Christians made up less than 1 percent of the population of the Roman Empire. We're talking about a time when, in an area with the population of Arkansas today, there would have been maybe a half-dozen churches, each about the size of our little congregation. We're talking about a time when over 99 percent of the population not only wasn't Christian but also wasn't accommodating to Christians. The vast majority of non-Christians tended to look askance at Christians and to be suspicious of their worship practices. Christians often were ridiculed for revering as divine a person who had been humiliated, tortured, and killed through crucifixion—which meant also: who had been executed as a criminal threat to Roman law and order and peace. Christians often were shunned on suspicion of having criminal minds. Christians often were scorned for lack of devotion to the emperor and for disloyalty to the state. Christians often were disdained for their refusal to honor the gods and the values the Romans long had honored. Christians often were looked down on as social deviants and frequently were blamed when misfortune happened to hit some part of the empire. It wasn't that all Christians always and everywhere suffered these things. Still, early Christians lived in a world that was antagonistic and even hostile to the cause of Jesus Christ. Persecution happened. Christians had to be ready to suffer the spite and resentment of the majority. They even had to be ready for execution. That's one reason those who did desire to join the church had to go through such a lengthy period of preparation before being allowed to become members—a period focused on nurturing the kind of courage, moral fortitude, and sense of community that were needed by all who would submit and commit to the lordship of Jesus Christ.

However, at least one characteristic of those early Christians met with mixed rather than with merely negative reactions, even among the church's critics. That characteristic was this: their *radical embrace of the life of love learned from Jesus*; their emphatic practice of altruistic, other-oriented, self-giving, even self-sacrificial love; their resolve, no matter how adverse the environment, to be known first and foremost by the love they showed to the loveless, the love they showed to those to whom the world had been unkind. That translated into this: giving priority to caring for the poor and needy, lifting up the destitute, tending to the sick and dying, practicing hospitality to strangers, generously sharing with the have-nots whatever possessions they themselves might have, and graciously giving of themselves to guard the dignity and bring about the well-being of those the world had passed by on the other side of the road. And early Christian love was aimed not only at other Christians, but at non-Christians as well, and without a thought of receiving anything in return. It was about loving others not on the basis of what you get but simply on the basis of what they need and what is yours to give.

In the Roman Empire, as in any culture where self-interest, possessiveness, competition, will to power, and the glorification of I-me-mine are the first order of the day, this Christian way of serving others seemed unusual, strange, bizarre. Over time, however, what may have done as much as anything else to enable the cause of the church to make early headway in its hostile environment was Christian love—love altruistically focused on the dignity and well-being of others, be they one's friends, be they one's enemies—love altruistically focused first, foremost, and above all on the dignity and well-being of those who've been denied dignity and well-being.

(3)

I want now to say what I believe those early Christians may well have heard when they heard what Jesus said at the end of his donkey ride into Jerusalem. I believe they may have heard something like the following: "This is going to sound strange to you, but," declares Jesus, "to follow me, you're going to have to learn to hate something that you feel you have a right to love enjoying. You have been enjoying life, you have been loving your life, by letting an emotional wall form itself between you and the ocean of troubles and woes that, at any given moment, haunt the world all around you. You've been enjoying life, you've been loving your life, forgetful of how surrounded you are by a world of sad and troubled and hurting people. Now, however, you must learn to *hate* that. You must learn to *hate* it when the blessings you enjoy are denied to other people. You must learn to *hate* the thought of living at an undisturbed distance from the troubles and needs of others. You must learn to *hate* it when you enjoy privileges that are denied to others. You must learn to *hate* the thought of not doing anything—or of not doing enough—to better and beautify the world of the sick, the hungry, the poor, the persecuted, the distressed, the lonely, the less privileged, the helpless, the unloved. And, you must learn to *love* helping others in their difficult times and desperate situations. You must learn to *love* doing what you can to improve the lives of others and to make this a better and more beautiful world for all people. You must learn to sense, when you look to others, that you cannot love your *own* life without loving *them* as well. *Do this*," those early Christians, I believe, heard Jesus say, "follow me in *this* way, and you will find yourself walking mysteriously hand in hand, shoulder to shoulder, and heart to heart, right here on Earth, with eternal God."

(4)

Jesus did not go to Jerusalem wanting to die. He knew that God created life good, and that God intends for us to receive and enjoy life as a precious gift. However, Jesus went to Jerusalem knowing also this: God wants us to sense, when we look to other people, that we cannot love ourselves without loving them as well; God wants us to hate it when the blessings we enjoy are denied to others; and God wants us to make this a better and more beautiful world for everyone.

To be sure, it is not easy figuring out what that means for us individually. After all, God desires for each of *us* to thrive and flourish; God desires for each of us to enjoy life in all its goodness and beauty. Moreover, the world is filled with more violence, injustice, oppression, cruelty, suffering, hunger, illness, and desperation than we as individuals can imagine taking on; the needs of others are finally so great, we simply cannot meet them all. So, how are we to know how much God wants us to enjoy from the world for ourselves, and how much of ourselves God wants us to give to others? The answer? It's hard to say!

We're not all called to make identical sacrifices. We're not all called to deny ourselves in precisely the same ways for Christ's sake. We are, however, all called by Jesus to learn to hate the thought of pulling back to a comfortable distance from the troubles and needs of others; to learn to hate it when the blessings we enjoy are denied to other people; to learn to hate it when we enjoy privileges that others can't; and to learn, in looking to others, to sense that we cannot love our own life without loving them as well.

You still won't always know just how much God wants you to enjoy from the world for yourself and how much of yourself God wants you to give to others. But you *will* be looking in the right direction—the direction of Jesus on his humble little donkey, riding passionately and compassionately into Jerusalem and into the heart of darkness; riding passionately and compassionately into a world of pain and suffering; riding passionately and compassionately into your life and my life with God's gift of life- and world-changing love. Amen.

Luke 23:50–24:12   Looking for the living.

April 12, 2020, Easter Sunday

Greeting
The grace of the Lord Jesus Christ be with you all!

Today is Easter Sunday. Let me say, here at the start, the single most important thing to be said today:

The Jesus with and through whose grace I greet you this day is the resurrected one!

Jesus's followers had lost him through death, yet they—and through them, now we—have been sought and found by Jesus as the resurrected one. Jesus is the crucified one. In the midst of a world that has fallen from God's good will and way, Jesus took up Israel's prophetic call to do justice, love kindness, and humbly embrace God's compassionately righteous ways. Jesus confronted and challenged forces hostile to the kingdom of God. Those forces, in turn, persecuted Jesus and killed him through the tortured humiliation of a crucifixion. But now God has *justified* Jesus's cause; God has *vindicated* how Jesus lived; God has *overturned* how Jesus died; and God has *declared* Jesus to be the one who speaks for God. God has done this by revealing Jesus as the *resurrected* one.

The world still is a fallen world, haunted by hostile and ungodly forces. Demonic passions and debilitating fears still plague this mortal life. Power keeps falling into arrogant and selfish hands. Poverty, hunger, and destitution assault us. Injury, illness, and death assail us. Hardship and hostility besiege us. Nevertheless, in the midst of all our fallenness, and amidst all the tragedy and pain, God has given us a glimpse of what God ultimately is up to with us. God has shown us and lifted us into God's power to redeem: God's power to draw all things—even all terrible and frightening things—into a future set free from what is contrary to the justice, peace, and love of God.

The resurrection of Jesus from the dead is the revelation of God's power and promise to redeem us from all ill and join us to life that is eternally beautiful, eternally good, eternally true. The once-crucified Jesus is the resurrected one! Neither life nor death can ever be the same again for any of us. Even while we live in this fallen world, we belong also already to a new age that is coming. We have been lifted into the world of the resurrection, where "neither death, nor life, nor angels, nor rulers, nor things present, nor things to come, nor powers, nor height, nor depth, nor anything else in all creation, will be able to separate us from the love of God." Christ is risen, risen indeed! And that is the single most important thing to be said today: *Jesus is the resurrected one!*

Please join me now in a moment of prayer, through words adapted from a prayer by Karl Barth, offered on an occasion such as today. Let us pray.

> Sovereign, heavenly God, you have humbled yourself in order to exalt us. Through your grace, free and unmer- ited, you came to us so that we might come to you. You took upon yourself our humanity in order to raise us up into eternal life. In the knowledge of this mystery and

this wonder, we come to praise you, and to proclaim and hear your word. We lack the wherewithal to do that unless you lift our hearts and minds to you. Be present now in our midst, we pray. Through your Holy Spirit, open for us the way to come to you, that we may see with our own eyes your light which has come into the world, and that, in the living of our lives, we may become your witnesses. Amen[5]

++++++++++++++++++++++++++++++++

Announcements

Let me introduce myself to any visitors we have joining us by video. I'm Ruskin Falls. I'm here in our sanctuary on a Friday afternoon, recording this service for broadcast this Easter Sunday. I'm joined by LaWanda Harris, who is our liturgist today; Sally Todd, our pianist; Ferris Allen, our soloist; and David Harper, our videographer.

In compliance with health and safety measures that the public has been asked to observe due to COVID-19, the session of our church decided to replace our public services of worship with video services. As far as know-how and experience at doing this sort of thing goes, we strictly started from scratch, and we still have a lot to learn. But we *are* learning, and we're giving it our best.

One thing we learned this week is that, due to lighting, the Easter lily arrangement that we usually have at the back of the chancel, right under the stained-glass window, doesn't show up

---

through the video camera we're using. So, we've set up a table of lilies here close to the pulpit, so they can be seen. The lilies were purchased with donations made by members in memory or in honor of someone special. On Wednesday we sent out a brochure listing those dedications. If you didn't get one but would like to receive a listing of dedications, let us know, and we'll send you one.

As with our first two video services, I hope that what we do here will serve to give us all a worshipful sense of *belonging together* this day and *belonging to God*.

+ +

Luke 23:50–24:12   *Looking for the living.*

TEXT *(English translation: NRSV)*

Now there was a good and righteous man named Joseph, who, though a member of the council, had not agreed to their plan and action. He came from the Jewish town of Arimathea, and he was waiting expectantly for the kingdom of God. This man went to Pilate and asked for the body of Jesus. Then he took it down, wrapped it in a linen cloth, and laid it in a rock-hewn tomb where no one had ever been laid. It was the day of Preparation, and the sabbath was beginning. The women who had come with him from Galilee followed, and they saw the tomb and how his body was laid. Then they returned, and prepared spices and ointments. On the sabbath they rested according to the commandment.

But on the first day of the week, at early dawn, they came to the tomb, taking the spices that they had prepared. They found the stone rolled away from the tomb, but when they went in, they did not find the body. While they were perplexed about this, suddenly two men in dazzling clothes stood beside them. The women were terrified and bowed their faces to the ground, but the men said to them, "Why do you look for the living among the dead? He is not here, but has risen. Remember how he told you, while he was still in Galilee, that the Son of Man must be handed over to sinners, and be crucified, and on the third day rise again." Then they remembered his words, and returning from the tomb, they told all this to the eleven and to all the rest. Now it was Mary Magdalene, Joanna, Mary the mother of James, and the other women with them who told this to the apostles. But these words seemed to them an idle tale, and they did not believe them. But Peter got up and ran to the tomb; stooping and looking in, he saw the linen cloths by themselves; then he went home, amazed at what had happened.

(1)

Clearly, they were expecting a corpse. Jesus, as well as the movement that he had been stirring up, was dead. So, his body should have been in the tomb. And they couldn't understand why it wasn't.

As Luke will go on to tell us in his second book, the Acts of the Apostles, it took forty days for Jesus's followers to come to realize that God had resurrected Jesus from the dead and to understand that God had done this in order to reveal to them Jesus's true identity—that God had done this to make known to them what they had failed to see and understand before, namely that the Jesus they had followed and then denounced, deserted, and denied is indeed—even and precisely as the crucified one— the Messiah, the Christ, the one chosen by God to manifest God's saving presence in the world and to reign as the Lord who reveals God's word and will and way.

It took time for all of that to sink in, and it came about in this way: over the course of forty days, the crucified Jesus would appear here and there to various followers, mysteriously alive; he would school them anew regarding his mission; then, equally mysteriously, he'd go silent and disappear from sight. Yet even as they experienced these appearances, followers weren't sure what to make of them. They weren't even sure that it actually was *Jesus* they were seeing. When we consider the Easter story in its entirety, we can tell that the disciples both did and didn't recognize the resurrected Jesus as the Jesus they had known before. Recognition of Jesus as the resurrected one and realization that the appearances were God's act of revealing Jesus's true identity as the Lord did not immediately dawn on them. The realization that Jesus, even and precisely in his suffering and dying, had come as the revealer of God's word and will and way didn't come about all at once, but only over time. But it did come. Through his resurrection appearances, Jesus brought his followers to see what, earlier, they had been blind to, namely that they had been called to testify throughout the world that Jesus is very God's own life-changing and world-changing word.

Over the course of forty days of resurrection appearances, Jesus reeducated his followers regarding his mission. Then he deemed them ready to carry on in his earthly absence. And then, as mysteriously as they had begun, the encounters with him ceased, and something new began to happen in Jesus's absence: followers began to experience his resurrection Spirit invisibly active among them, teaching them how to live and work together as the community they came to call Christ's church.

This gathering of the community of Christ's resurrection Spirit became how and where the identity and mission of Jesus continued to announce itself in the world. With the formation of the church, the hearing and heeding of God's word no longer depended on resurrection appearances by Jesus. Rather, it now happened through the invisible presence of his Holy Spirit working in and through the life of this new community. It happened as the Holy Spirit used people's participation in the church to create in them eyes and ears for the crucified Jesus as the living Lord who speaks for God.

And that means this: Jesus founded the church to be how and where, in the future, people shall be brought into encounter with God's word. He founded the church to be how and where the word of God that he came revealing would go on revealing itself through his resurrection Spirit. Jesus founded the church to be how and where, even in his physical absence, his resurrection Spirit would go on opening hearts and minds to the word and will and way of God. It had been through Jesus's resurrection appearances that his earliest followers had been confronted with Jesus's true identity and turned into hearers and doers of God's word. Now, it would be in and through the church that later followers, such as you and me, would be confronted with Jesus's true identity and turned into hearers and doers of God's word.

The church, in other words, is a way of being together—it is a way of listening and speaking together; it is a way of praying and singing together; it is a way of sharing bread and wine together; it is a way of serving others; it is a way of coming before God and relating to one another—through which the Holy Spirit gives us eyes and ears for Jesus as God's own word, breaking into our lives to point the way to the future that God intends for all the world.

(3)

In that light, on this Easter Sunday, I want to make the following suggestion: we present-day Christians will do well to keep before us the question that the women in Luke's gospel found themselves being asked as they stood there at Jesus's empty tomb: "Why do you look for the living among the dead?"

Admittedly, we today know better than to look for Jesus among the dead in the way his first followers did. We know better than to seek his body in a tomb. We today already commemorate Easter as the event of his resurrection. Still, let me ask: when we commemorate Easter, where do we actually look for the resurrected Jesus?

For starters, we look to the past. We look to the first Easter. We look to the empty tomb. We recall that Jesus appeared to followers as the resurrected one, and that those followers began spreading the good news of the risen Jesus Christ.

If, however, we leave it at that, then Easter now is over. If we leave it at that, Easter has become, so to speak, a dead fact of history, something that is not a part of our own lived experience, but only an event commemorated as having happened once upon a time.

Yet, that way of looking at things misses the real Easter. For the real Easter is more than an over-and-done event that we collectively recall. The real Easter is something that happens to us *here and now*, in the lived experience of Christ's church. The real Easter is the event in which we find ourselves becoming opened to Jesus's true identity as Lord. The real Easter is the event in which we find ourselves being given new eyes and ears for Jesus breaking into our lives to point the way to the future that God intends for all the world. And just as the resurrection appearances were how and where this event happened for the first followers of Jesus, so the church is how and where that happens for us today.

In returning Jesus as the resurrected one to the world that crucified him, God unveiled, God revealed, God made known to disciples Jesus's true identity and mission. And, in that knowledge, they became the rock on which the Holy Spirit would build the church that would be for future followers what the resurrection appearances had been in the beginning, namely how and where it would be unveiled, revealed, made known, that the Jesus whom our world crucified is the living Lord of all.

That should tell us this: Easter is not just an event of the past. Easter is here and now! Easter is what is happening in and through the church when our listening and speaking, our praying and singing, our sharing of bread and wine, our service to others, our presence before God and with one another, all gets taken up into the Holy Spirit's activity of teaching us Jesus's true identity as Lord of all, who spoke and speaks for God.

And don't forget: it took more than just a single resurrection appearance for followers to grasp this. The appearances did not first fill his followers with certainty regarding Jesus. Rather, the appearances put them soundly on the path of *faith seeking understanding*. It was only as they wrestled with and learned from Jesus's appearances, that they came to realize that this was *God* at work, turning them into the community that was to become for future followers what the resurrection appearances had been for them, namely how and where people are awakened to Jesus's true identity and turned into hearers and doers of God's word.

Easter didn't just happen once upon a time. Easter is what happens whenever Christ's Holy Spirit takes this way of being together that we call the church and uses it to open us and to hold us open to Jesus as God's own word. Easter is what happens when the Holy Spirit takes this way of listening and speaking together—this way of praying and singing together, this way of sharing bread and wine together, this way of serving others, this way of coming before God and relating to one another—and uses all that to open us to Jesus himself breaking into our lives and taking hold of us as the way to the future that God intends for all the world. Whenever and wherever that happens, it is Easter. When and where the Holy Spirit opens us to Jesus's true identity and sparks among us faith seeking understanding, we know that his tomb was empty and that he is the resurrected one. Easter isn't just God's past act of raising Jesus from the dead. Easter is the Holy Spirit's present act of lifting people into true knowledge of Jesus Christ.

Whenever we catch wind of the Spirit sweeping across the baptismal font and the communion table; whenever we catch wind of the Spirit sounding forth through the proclamation of scripture, and through prayers said and sung, and even through our reverent silence; whenever we catch wind of the Spirit opening us and holding us open to the lordship of Jesus Christ and to the guidance and direction he gives, it is Easter. Breathing these winds of the Spirit, we know that the tomb is empty and that Christ is risen.

Easter, you see, never ended. It still is going on in Christ's church, whenever hearts are lifted, minds stretched, and wills girded by the Holy Spirit, disclosing to us Jesus's true identity and turning us into hearers and doers of God's word.

(4)

Which brings me to the question I shared with the congregation earlier this week: what does it mean to be Christ's church in the time of COVID-19? What does it mean to be the church where, in most cases, the compassionate thing to do is to keep our physical distance from each other and to cease gathering in our sanctuary and our fellowship hall and to stop visiting one another face to face—and this precisely in a moment of profound crisis for our families, our circles of friends, our health-care system and workers, our public servants and institutions, and our economy, incomes, and livelihoods? What does it mean to be Christ's church in such a time as this? We have no playbook for how to do this. We are learning on the go.

In any case, however, no matter what and come what may, we will do well to take to heart and keep always in mind that, in returning Jesus as the resurrected one to the world that crucified him, God has justified Jesus's cause, God has vindicated how Jesus lived, God has overturned how Jesus died, and God has declared that Jesus's life, Jesus's mission, Jesus's ever compassionately gracious love truly point the way to the future that is God's aim for all the world.

And that should give us confidence to declare to the world: It is God's doing that Christ is risen. His resurrection grounds our hope in the day that is coming when God at last shall redeem all the tragedy that haunts our world and all the folly that we harbor in our own hearts. His resurrection grounds our faith in God to one day transform whatever doesn't express God's love into the purest possible reflection of God's loving aims and purposes. His resurrection grounds our trust that the way of compassion is not a fool's errand that cuts us off from the good life, but instead is our participation in precisely the life that brings out in us what is most real and true and lastingly good about us. His resurrection grounds our courage to carry on in peace, with serenity of spirit and a knowing smile, even in the face of all that is confusing, intimidating, painful, and hard. His resurrection lifts us up into his Holy Spirit, in whose fellowship, here on Earth, we walk hand in hand, shoulder to shoulder, and heart to heart with Jesus himself, and in whose fellowship, beyond this Earth, we shall glorify and fully enjoy God forever. Christ is risen. It is God's doing. By God's grace we have been saved and now are called to do God's goodness justice.

Amen.

(8)

Jeremiah 17:5–8   Desert stream.

April 19, 2020, 2nd Sunday of Easter

Greeting
The grace of the Lord Jesus Christ be with you all!

Today is the second Sunday of Easter. You may have thought that Easter consists of a single Sunday, and that it was seven days ago. However, on the traditional worship calendar of the church, in what we call the Christian year, the whole forty-nine-day period from Easter Sunday until Pentecost Sunday is celebrated as the Season of Easter.

The church traditionally has intended this to be for us a season of worship in which, week by week, we let ourselves become more genuinely aware of and more soundly reshaped in our identity as God's Easter people—people who know themselves drawn into God's gracious and holy presence through the history of Jesus Christ—which includes the history of the law and the prophets of Israel, the history of the crucifixion and resurrection of Jesus, and the history of the work of his resurrection Spirit through the community we now call the church.

It belongs to my prayer that, through this service of worship, sound guidance shall come our way. Amen.

✝ ✝

81

Announcements

I'm not used to introducing myself to the congregation. However, in doing this particular worship service as a video without a bulletin identifying who's here doing what, and realizing it's possible that joining us right now, there may be some people who don't know who we are, I'll do some introducing. I'm Ruskin Falls, and I serve as minister for Pulaski Heights Presbyterian Church. In this time of social distancing, there are just three other members of our church family with me here. LaWanda Harris is serving once again as our liturgist. Sally Todd, who serves as music director for our church, is our pianist. And David Harper is making the video.

Although we are prerecording this service on a Friday afternoon, it is slated to begin running on our website at ten forty-five Sunday morning, which is the time we ordinarily begin our Sunday service together. (I think on the website that's called our "premiere showing.") I hope that doing it this way helps us on Sunday to feel a little more gathered together spiritually than we can be right now physically.

We'll then leave the video up on our website, accessible to anyone who wants to view it. It will stay up until next Friday afternoon, when we'll take it down to make room for a new worship video, which in turn will become accessible (in video lingo: will *premiere*) at ten forty-five the following Sunday morning.

We don't know how much longer the COVID-19 pandemic is going to require that we do our worshiping at a "social distance." We don't know just when or by what degrees it's going to become safe being physically close again. And even after it's actually deemed safe to be together again the way we were before, we don't know how long it's going to be before we actually feel just as normal and just as safe being close to each other as we did before. And we don't know just how financially stressful and even disastrous and even ruinous this is going to be for how many people before it's over. And we don't know just how many are going to get sick—and how many are going to die—before we can talk about the COVID-19 outbreak in the past tense. This new coronavirus has filled our lives and homes and world with a quite unexpected kind of uncertainty and anxiety and anguish. The situation demands of us lots of patience, understanding, goodwill, kindness, trust, resilience, and courage.

I hope and pray that what we offer here in the way of a time of divine worship will be of help to us all in taking on the demands of the time of COVID-19, as well as in taking on any and all other demands this world of troubles and woes may send our way.

+ +

Jeremiah 17:5–8   *Desert stream.*

TEXT *(English translation: NRSV)*
> Thus says the LORD:
> Cursed are those who trust in mere mortals and make mere flesh their strength, whose hearts turn away from the LORD. They shall be like a shrub in the desert, and shall not see when relief comes. They shall live in the parched places of the wilderness, in an uninhabited salt land.
> Blessed are those who trust in the LORD, whose trust is the LORD. They shall be like a tree planted by

water, sending out its roots by the stream. It shall not fear when heat comes, and its leaves shall stay green; in the year of drought it is not anxious, and it does not cease to bear fruit.

(1)

You can be a shrub in the desert, declares the prophet Jeremiah, living in the parched places of the wilderness. Or you can be a tree planted by water, sending out its roots by the stream.

I invite you to ponder Jeremiah's words by thinking about the geography of the American West. Of course, what we are likely to think about first—and what we can imagine ourselves going there to see—are the mountains, canyons, and other fantastic geological formations the West is famous for. I've been out west, and I will say that there is some amazing scenery to behold. There are great expanses of enormous stone shapes and figures; there are towering cliffs; there are high, sweeping plateaus; there are places where the land drops off stunningly deeply into immensely wide canyons ripping through the earth. There are, indeed, breathtaking geological formations worth going out west to see. The wilderness scenery there can fill your eyes with amazement.

And, there is a lot of wilderness out there—lots of desert-like wilderness. Sometimes for as far as the eye can see, there's just a vast expanse of rocks and more rocks atop dry, rocky, crusty ground, without much of anything at all in the way of greenery. Such a landscape is not a hospitable dwelling place for plants. Still, though, it's a landscape filled with fascinating and intriguing marvels of earth and stone.

What I want you to ponder with me this morning, however, is not those spellbinding marvels. What I want us to ponder today is something I don't believe anyone here in Arkansas is going to travel all the way out west just to see. Yet, it was one of the most wonderful and amazing sites I saw while I was there. It was a little river. At least on the map it was called a river. Actually, it was more what I'd call a tiny stream. It was a little rolling stream I came upon one day while driving along a road that traversed a desert-like wilderness.

Before I came upon that stream of water, all I'd seen all around me had been the brown and red and orange colors of rocks and cliffs and dry, crusty ground. To be sure, there were some small plants as well, but they weren't much to speak of. Then, to my surprise, suddenly, in the middle of nowhere, I came upon this rolling stream of water.

For many yards on both sides of the stream, everything was green—and not just green, but lusciously green. There was soft grass; there were flowers; and there were real trees. And I don't mean some scraggly excuse for a tree, but real trees. Indeed: *fruit trees*! There were orchards of fruit trees planted there beside that stream. There, in the midst of a dry, rocky, and crusty wilderness, I saw this small rolling stream of water, and along its banks were trees that, year after year, flourish with blossom and flower and the bearing of fruit.

And now, whenever I read the passage we're listening to today from the book of Jeremiah, I think of that stream of water. I think of what an amazing difference I saw there between what sends its roots out by that stream and what tries to grow in a desert wilderness at a distance from that stream.

(2)

Let me note that I do believe that you have to respect any plant
that can stay alive in a desert environment. Desert shrubs don't
have it easy. They have all they can handle, just holding their
own. They have no dependable source of water. Constantly
threatened with the possibility of not enough rain, their
situation is always precarious. It's a wonder that they survive at
all. But they do! And that impresses me. Their life amazes me.

Yet, there is something grudging and restricted about their
life. Though they manage amazingly to stay alive, desert shrubs
don't thrive and flourish and prosper like those trees I saw
along the banks of that stream. The trees along that stream
are exuberant and bounteous. They widen and reach out their
branches, as if for love of the sun. They show no signs of fear
that they might run out of life. They yield luscious fruit season
after season without fear of becoming depleted or empty. And
as they reach upward and outward and produce fruit to give,
there's something else they do: they add unexpected beauty to
the world around them.

By comparison with those trees, the lives of desert shrubs
appear stingy and small. Desert shrubs must worry about
where the next rain is coming from and when. They must
conserve what they have for themselves. They don't dare stretch
themselves too much or get very far from the ground, as that
probably would mean their death. So, they do survive. They
hang on to life. But their life has to be small. Their life can't
be too generous. They must stay focused on their need for rain
and on how little rain there is to be had.

There is, of course, life in both places, even interesting life.
Desert life greatly distanced from any river still is not dull. It has

its excitement. It has its allurements. It yields its satisfactions. It's not just about anxiety and anguish. And there *are* days when the rains come, and things feel good.

Moreover, life beside that rolling stream isn't just a piece of cake. The temperatures that beat down on the desert shrubs beat down also on the trees beside that stream. The winds that howl across the desert shrubs howl across these trees as well. The nights get just as dark beside the stream as they do everywhere else in the desert.

Yet, what a world of difference there is between the desert shrub whose life is focused on how little rain there is and the tree that finds itself planted by water and, so, sends out its roots by the stream! Jeremiah would have us see that our lives can be like that desert shrub, or like that tree. And what spells the difference is this: where we put our ultimate trust. If, declares Jeremiah, we put it in mere mortals and make mere flesh our strength, we're going to live like a desert shrub that is focused on how little rain there is and not knowing when the next rain is coming. But if we put our ultimate trust in the Lord, if we truly trust in eternal God, creator of the heavens and the Earth, we can live like a tree planted by water, unafraid of becoming depleted or empty, but instead yielding fruit to give away.

(3)

Let's back up a step.

God created the world to let other beings enjoy and share in the goodness that God is. Creation does, however, include things that are perplexing and even anguishing. It includes hardship, disappointment, and defeat. It includes illness and injury. It includes suffering and death. Such things as these keep us worried and insecure. They concern, they trouble, they frighten us. They fill us with anxiety and anguish regarding the meaning of our life, regarding what our life should be about, regarding our value and worth in this world, and regarding the meaning of death and what becomes of us when we die.

Pressed upon by this anxiety and anguish, we strive to secure ourselves against it. We strive to obtain for ourselves things and relationships and positions and experiences that we trust to satisfy our need for meaning, purpose, self-worth, self-esteem, and security.

However, we never seem to get enough of what we feel we need; we never get from the things and relationships and positions and experiences that we have, what we finally need to feel as secure as we think we need to feel. And, so, we keep striving for more. We keep striving for what we trust will finally allay our anxiety and anguish. We keep striving to acquire things, to have experiences, to obtain positions, and to find relationships that will finally make us feel secure. But we never get enough. We never feel finally satisfied. Peace and security never finally settle into our souls. We keep striving for more. We never feel we have enough knowledge, or enough things, or enough experiences, or enough understanding, respect, appreciation, and love from others, to cease our striving. In fact, we become dominated by a sense—indeed, by a kind of fear—of not enough: fear of not enough purpose and meaning; fear of not enough recognition and acknowledgment; fear of not enough prosperity; fear of not enough security; fear of not enough control; fear of not enough understanding; fear of not enough accomplishment; fear of not enough affection; fear of not enough love; fear of not enough health; fear of not enough time.

And that's what turns us into desert shrubs. Fear-of-not-enough centers us in a very narrow way on our own self and on what we think we need and deserve for ourselves. Dominated by fear of not enough, we become ensnared, entangled, and imprisoned in our own frantic striving to secure life for ourselves. Fear-of-not-enough focuses us narrowly on our own will in competition—in sometimes callous competition—with other wills, striving for whatever it is that we believe will finally give us the security we think we need and deserve. Fear-of-not-enough leads us to clutch tightly to and circle the wagons around I-me-mine. Fear-of-not-enough turns us into hoarders of whatever we believe will finally make us feel safe. It leaves us living like a desert shrub that can't be safe without staying centered on how little rain there is.

If, on the other hand, declares Jeremiah, you find yourself planted by the waters of the Lord—if you live with your roots sent out by *that* stream—you need not let yourself be ruled by fear of not enough. For beside those waters you know that you can trust God to have always and only your and your world's truly best interests at heart and to be ever at work in your life to fit you and ready you for the future that God is calling into being.

Recognition that we have been planted beside the streaming waters of eternal God nurtures in us a trust in God in which we grow to see that we need not fear any evil, that we need not be afraid of losing ourselves, and that we can dare more beautiful things and far greater generosity than we otherwise ever would have ventured. Trusting in the Lord, when the heat does come, our leaves shall stay green; trusting in the Lord, in time of drought, we won't need to be anxious or stop bearing fruit for others. Planted beside the streaming waters of eternal

God, we can—no matter what and come what may!—lead a life that radiates *serene courage*.

(4)

Note well, trusting in the Lord doesn't mean you're never worried, confused, or scared. It doesn't mean you never know fear. Rather, it means that, deep down—deep down around your *spiritual roots*—you are always in touch with good reason *not* to be afraid. It means that, deep down, your very sense of who you are includes awareness of your life as a gift from and as the graciously loving concern of eternal God. And, so, in all circumstances, whatever happens and come what may, you know yourself mysteriously, wonderfully safe. In that awareness, even when you find yourself afraid of something, fear's grip on you becomes looser and weaker than otherwise, and you become more free. You know you no longer *need* to be afraid because you're planted beside the waters of God's abiding love. Your roots are by God, who loves you beyond your imagination and forever. You don't need to be afraid because you realize that you're never more than a prayer away from the God who is determined to redeem your life from any and every pit that you could ever, ever, fall into.

There *are* things in this life that are going to confuse and frighten us. There *are* things that can shake us hard with fear and maybe even terror. However, when our life is rooted in trust in God, that trust really does create in us a courage that is unlike anything the world itself could ever give—a bravery, a boldness, a daring, that is tranquil, composed, and serene, and that, even when things are happening to or around us that shoot fear into our souls, doesn't close us off to the needs of others, but holds us open to their needs and to what is ours to give.

Fear *can* shake *any* of us hard. We may be feeling bold and brave right now, but there are things that can shake us to our core with fear. Trusting in God means that even the fear that shakes us to our core stops at our roots. Trusting in God means that, whatever fear does to us at first, we know our roots are by eternal God. Deep down in our roots, we know that we belong to the God whose loving concern for us and gracious watchfulness over us never ceases. Deep down we know that when we are afraid, and even when we're terrified, we have good reason to say to ourselves, "I am mysteriously, wonderfully safe!" That doesn't mean no worldly harm can reach us, but it does mean this: no harm can reach us that is stronger than God's desire and promise to redeem us from all ill, to redeem us from all evil, to redeem us from all suffering, to redeem us from all ungodliness, so that we might thrive and flourish and give of ourselves as eternal God's eternally beloved children.

Blessed are those who trust in the Lord, whose trust is in the Lord. They shall be like a tree planted by water, sending out its roots by the stream. Amen.

(9)

Romans 8:28　How the world looks to those who love God.

April 26, 2020, 3rd Sunday of Easter

Greeting
The grace of the Lord Jesus Christ be with you all!

Today is the third Sunday of Easter, Easter (or Eastertide) being a season of worship on the Christian calendar that is intended especially to help us become reminded of and reshaped in our identity as God's Easter people, which is to say people who have found ourselves joined by the crucified but resurrected Jesus to the promises, purposes, and aims that our eternally loving God is working out in the world—and joined as well to the tasks that God, in Christ, has given us.

The fact of the matter is this: this world that God so loves—this world that the God who *is* love eternally loves—this world that eternal God created so that other beings might know, enjoy, and share God's love—is, beyond our understanding, a world haunted by ailments, injuries, heartbreaks, storms, wars, madness, cruelty, injustice, and yet other misfortunes and tragedies. Right now, we find ourselves haunted by a pandemic brought on by the new coronavirus. And yet, on any given day—on any given day *prior* to the outbreak of COVID-19, as still will be the case on any given day after this outbreak at last subsides—there are neighborhoods, villages, cities, even countries, and sometimes regions of this world, that have been turned into sites of hardship, calamity, disaster, sorrow, and suffering.

As God's Easter people, we are called not to try to distance ourselves from that fact, but to keep it constantly, prayerfully on our hearts and minds, together with this question: what is ours—and what is mine—to do this day, for the sake of God's love for the world?

Easter people are those who find themselves enabled through Jesus Christ to see others as children of eternal God's graciously redeeming love, and, in that light, to attend to others' deepest needs in all life's joys and through all life's trials.

It belongs to my prayer that this service of worship shall help us to become more nearly, dearly, and clearly attuned to God's love and to the courage that God desires for us to have and to inspire in others. Amen.

+ +

Announcements

Due to the health measures we've been asked to take in response to the outbreak of COVID-19, only four of our members are here in the sanctuary today: Charles Gray is here as our liturgist. Sally Todd is our pianist. David Harper is our videographer. And I'm Ruskin Falls. I'll be doing the preaching.

So, there's just the four of us here. And yet I would not describe this place as empty. This place truly is for our church family a *sanctuary*, the very meaning of which is "sacred space." And sacred spaces are not empty.

I like the way Daniel Frankforter says it in his book, *Stones for Bread*:

> An authentic sanctuary...feels different from an ordinary room. It has a kind of majesty. This is not an effect of architectural design or artistic decoration, but a glow from the patina of use. What gives a sanctuary the characteristic stillness of a holy place is the fact that it has been kept apart from the world and respected as the arena for the most serious of human undertakings, the approach to God.

> Crude or basic buildings are well able to radiate holiness. The clapboard structures that Southern sharecroppers erected with their own hands, many smaller rural and urban churches, and even some city "storefronts" succeed in proclaiming respect for the dignity of worship.

> To be consecrated by and for worship a building need not be elaborate, but it must have integrity. It must proclaim its people's belief that what they do within it is important enough to deserve the best that they can provide. This may mean soaring vaults and gold chalices or log cabins and clay cups. What is important is not the value, but the commitment to honor God.[6]

Even though only four of us are physically present, this place is not empty. A history of commitment to honor God fills

---

[6] A. Daniel Frankforter, *Stones for Bread: A Critique of Contemporary Worship* (Louisville: Westminster John Knox Press, 2001), 156, 159, 160.

this room, even now. And however far apart you and I are geographically in this moment, to have experienced this place as sanctuary is to know that we share a mysterious togetherness here right now. This place isn't empty. You are here. And we have work to do together—the work of serving the word of the Lord our God.

+ +

Romans 8:28   *How the world looks to those who love God.*

TEXT *(English translation: NRSV)*
>   We know that all things work together for good
>   for those who love God, who are called according to
>   his purpose.

(1)

That's one line from a letter the apostle Paul wrote to the Christians in Rome. He was in Greece when he wrote the letter, and he was giving thought to traveling to Spain to get new churches up and running there. And he was thinking that perhaps the Christians in Rome would be willing to serve as a home base for that mission and provide financial assistance for carrying it out. Paul eventually did make it to Rome. He arrived, however, not as a missionary on his way to Spain, but as a prisoner on his way, it turned out, to his execution. Paul's way of following Jesus had put him criminally at odds with the social order of the powers that be in the Roman Empire, and he paid for that with his life. Here, though, in this letter, his hopes are high for going to Spain—as is his confidence that all things work together for good for those who love God.

(2)

Paul is *not* saying that God works only for the good of those who love God and not for the good of those who live turned away from God. After all, years before, back when Paul first experienced the resurrected Jesus calling to him, what he experienced was Jesus laying bare just how horribly turned away from God Paul's own life really was. In that vision of the resurrected Jesus, Paul heard himself being condemned by eternal God for leading a life sinfully and oh-so self-righteously at odds with God. At the very same time, however, he heard God forgiving him his sin and redeeming and fitting him for life as a servant of the gospel of Jesus—the gospel, he came to see, of God's unconditional love and redeeming grace. Paul came out of that experience knowing that the resurrection of Jesus was God's way of revealing the truth regarding human sinfulness and regarding God's forgiveness and how far God's forgiveness goes. He came out of it realizing how tragically entangled in sin we humans are—how tragically entangled we are in resistance to the world that God intends—and how determined God is to set us free and transform our world.

That also had been the lesson of Jesus's earliest disciples. In the end, they themselves had doubted, denied, and deserted Jesus, and they had forsaken his cause. When he then was crucified, they were left to live with their misgivings, guilt, and shame. Yet, precisely in that situation, Jesus came to them as the resurrected one, embracing them as his still-beloved friends and tenderly rejoining them to his cause.

In Jesus's return to them as the resurrected one, those disciples heard Jesus declaring as God's own word to them, "For all that you have gotten so terribly and tragically wrong,

I forgive you." That Jesus came to them the way he did as the resurrected one was, for them, an incredible act of God and the sign of an incredible wideness in God's mercy. It was an amazing sign of God's amazing grace toward the frightened and the faithless. As a result, the disciples' anxiety and shame became replaced by tranquility and trust. They now knew that, no matter how far the world might stray from God's ways, what God is up to in this world has always and only to do with God's unconditional love and redeeming grace; God's work in this world has always and only to do with bringing out in us what God knows is truly best about us, and being for us the God of our salvation.

We can even put it this way: the first lesson that Jesus's followers learned from their experiences of his return to them as the resurrected one following his crucifixion was that Jesus's life and mission truly was God at work laying bare humanity's sinful attitude toward God and revealing God's graciously loving attitude toward humanity. The first lesson they learned was this: we humans have turned the world into and tolerated it as a place of ungodly arrogance, injustice, and violence; yet God has created the world as the object of eternal love, and God does not do anything that is not an act of eternal love.

(3)

I realize that there are passages in the Bible where we are given to ponder the likes of particular wars, storms, and diseases as punishment for someone having angered God. However, such passages are to be read in their historical context and in the light of what is at the heart of Holy Scripture, which is this: God's self-revelation as the creator and redeemer who relates to us first, foremost, and always through a compassionate, merciful, forgiving—indeed unconditional—love that neither seeks nor needs satisfaction through revenge or retribution. Jesus, in whom God's love was revealed in human flesh, came, as the Gospel of John puts it, not to condemn the world but to save it. He captured our human hearts and minds by loving us even at the cost of his own life and then returning as the resurrected one to forgive the world what it had done and to breathe a new beginning into life on Earth. And that's what God does for us all. God does not work less lovingly with some people than with others. God is for everyone the God of compassionate, merciful, forgiving, and unconditionally redeeming love.

That doesn't mean we are not judged by God. It simply means that we, all of us, are judged by God's love. Yes, God holds us accountable for all the unloving and all the less-than-loving things we do. However, God can, does, and will hold us accountable, never for the sake of revenge or retribution, but always and only for love's sake and, so, with our and our world's truly best interests truly, lovingly at heart.

And note well: love's way is not the way of coercive force. God is not out to force the world into the future that God intends, but to *love* the world into that future. God is working God's aims and purposes out in this world, not through coercive force but through the persuasive power of God's graciously redeeming love.

And that means this: not everything that happens, happens as God's will. It means we cannot and must not point to occurrences of violence, injustice, injury, disease, or other suffering, and insist that that's God's will. Rather, *amidst* everything that happens to and around us, God is always lovingly with us, teaching us to *draw forth* something good and godly *from* all that. God is always with us and for us, plying us with the faith, hope, love, and courage we need, to draw forth, even from sad and tragic things, consequences that aren't merely sad and tragic—consequences that actually serve some good that moves the world a little closer to, rather than yet farther from, the future God's love intends.

The fact is, God lets humanity go its way and even suffer the tragic consequences of some of its ways, without intervening to *force* things in God's direction. But, to say that God *doesn't intervene* to stop something from happening doesn't mean that God willed it to happen as it did. Rather, it means that the God of unconditional love stops short of *manipulating* us, stops short of *forcing* God's will upon us, stops short of *coercing* us into being the persons and world that God desires. God has created a world whose life God desires to let unfold *without* divine coercion and, so, *without* turning us into puppets who can do only what God would have us do. God doesn't use *coercion* to get us to do God's will. Rather, God moves us through the *persuasive* power of God's love for the world—the persuasive power that has walked among us in the life and mission of Jesus—the Jesus whom this world crucified, but whom God returned to the world, declaring, "I love you, still! Now, come, follow me!"

To be sure, God's love works in a way that remains mysterious to us. We can't say exactly how God's love gets through to our often-anxious souls, to our often-hardened hearts, to our often-stubborn wills. Nevertheless, in the light of the gospel of Jesus, we can say that God always *is* lovingly at work to give us direction, so that, whatever happens, however sad or tragic a particular event itself might be, we can turn it toward ends that are not merely sad and tragic, but that serve God's good and loving purposes. God always is mysteriously at work with us, stretching our minds and lifting our spirits into the revelation of God's goodness, grace, and creative aim; God is unceasingly near to us all, breathing into us the faith, hope, love, and courage we need for discerning and doing what needs to be done, to make this world more like the world intended by God's love. God is always with us to help us draw forth even from the worst of situations a path that leads to something good. God doesn't force our hands, but God does speak to our hearts and minds in divinely persuasive ways, enabling us to turn even bad things into a better tomorrow.

(4)

It is in this sense that those who love God see all things working together for good.

As we learn to love the purposes that God, through Jesus, has declared God's own, we learn, along with our worries and fears, also to trust God to continue working those purposes out in our present lives and beyond. We receive new eyes and ears for recognizing that, in all that happens—no matter how troubling or how horrible or how sad—God is with us to show us how to turn our situation toward something good, to show us how to turn our situation toward something that shines with the justice, peace, and redeeming grace of God's coming kingdom. As you learn to love what God is up to in the life and mission of Jesus, you receive, not certainty about the details of God's activity among us in any given moment, but trust in

God's good purposes and in God's mysterious way of working out those purposes, in and with and through your life.

That is why Christian faith isn't wishful thinking about the future. Christian faith is not about fantasizing a future that will accord with your wants, wishes, and desires. Christian faith is an actual experience. It is an experience of being confronted by a power that is outside of you—a power that is different from your own wants, wishes, and desires. Christian faith is an experience of Christ's resurrection Spirit confronting you with the wants, the wishes, the desires of eternal God. It's about finding your wants, wishes, and desires confronted and challenged and reshaped by the gospel—the good news of the justice, peace, and redeeming grace of the kingdom of God that Jesus proclaimed and served. Christian faith is about learning to love and become changed by the purposes that we, through the life and mission of Jesus, have learned to see and hear God working out in the world.

Christian faith is a response to an unseen presence that is outside our own selves. It's a response to the Spirit of the crucified yet resurrected Jesus, reaching out to us through the scriptures, preaching, sacraments, and fellowship of the community that Spirit created—the community we call the church. Christian faith is about becoming enabled to trust the future to the God of the crucified yet resurrected Jesus. Christian faith is about growing, day by day and little by little, to trust the God who, through Jesus, confronts, challenges, and reshapes our lives even now, with a justice, peace, and redeeming grace that are not of this world, but that nevertheless are the God-ordained future of this world.

Christian faith is not certainty; it is faith. But it is not irrational or blind faith. It is not without ground and reason. It is the experience of the Spirit of Jesus giving us new eyes and ears for the reality, truth, and presence of God among us, calling into being a future that is far, far different than are the ways and means of this old world we're living in right now. Christian faith is the experience of Jesus giving us gospel eyes and ears for the reality, truth, and presence of God, guiding us toward and into the future that God's eternally unconditional love intends.

Thus it was that the apostle Paul could say—and that we can now say with him—*All things work together for good for those who love God.* Amen.

10

Hosea 1:9b–10; 2:14–15   Our infinitely good task.

May 3, 2020, 4th Sunday of Easter

Greeting
The grace of the Lord Jesus Christ be with you all!

On the calendar of the Christian year, we're in what the church calls the season of Easter. Easter is a seven-week season of worship intended especially to help us become reminded of and reshaped in our identity as God's resurrection people, so that we may proclaim and show more truly and with increasing courage the gospel of Jesus Christ our Lord.

It's easy to forget or fail to see, but the truth is this: we need to know eternal God's guidance, grace, and love if we are to know the world in all its fullness, enjoy life at its utmost best, and look death in the face with humbly undaunted courage. Christian worship is a way of being taught and constantly reminded to let ourselves be led by the wonderful—though also mysterious—God who reaches out to us through the history of Jesus Christ, including the history of the law and the prophets of Israel, and the history of the community of his resurrection Spirit, which we call the church.

It belongs to my prayer on this fourth Sunday of Easter that this service of worship shall help us all become more nearly, dearly, and clearly attuned to the mystery and goodness of God, and to the courage that God desires for us to have and to inspire in others. Amen.

+ +

Announcements

In case we have any visitors joining us for this service, I'll introduce myself. I'm Ruskin Falls, and I serve as minister here. With me in our sanctuary today are four other members of our church family. Serving as liturgist today is LaWanda Harris. Playing the piano and the organ is Sally Todd. Leading us in vocal singing is Mary Kai Clark. And doing the videography work is David Harper.

Church members may be surprised that we are using the organ today, as it has, for a long time now, been so much in need of extensive repair and renovation work that we simply haven't used it. But Sally wants to give it a try this morning. She is, as she said to me, "experimenting with a piece that will be more forgiving in navigating some of the current issues with our organ." And it's always good having Mary Kai here, helping to lift us all into the music of worship.

Tomorrow, Monday, May 4, Governor Hutchinson is scheduled to make an announcement regarding the possibility of soon lifting restrictions here in Arkansas on gatherings in places of worship. When a date is set for lifting those restrictions, our session still will need to determine whether that, or perhaps a later date, would make the most sense for our own congregation. And we will keep you informed.

For now, the five of us are coming to you socially distanced yet virtually near. Let us be glad for what, in this respect, our small congregation has been able to do to continue its services of worship in this difficult time.

+ +

Hosea 1:9b–10; 2:14–15   *Our infinitely good task.*

TEXT *(English translation: NRSV)*

  Then [regarding the house of Israel] the Lord said, "You are not my people and I am not your God." Yet the number of the people of Israel shall be like the sand of the sea, which can be neither measured nor numbered; and in the place where it was said to them, "You are not my people," it shall be said to them, "Children of the living God."

  Therefore, I will now allure her, and bring her into the wilderness, and speak tenderly to her. From there I will give her her vineyards, and make the Valley of Achor a door of hope. There she shall respond as in the days of her youth, as at the time when she came out of the land of Egypt.

(1)

The situation that Hosea saw was this: the world that the God of goodness, grace, and love intends for humanity to enjoy and share in keeping with God's creative aim has come to be dominated by ungodly forces of arrogance and greed, injustice and indifference, violence and fear, oppression and suffering. God is out to restore in this world, the life that God intends. God is out to do this by letting the world get to know God truly. Toward that end, God formed Israel to be a people who would dwell in incredibly intimate nearness to God's own word and will and way. At the center of what Israel was to learn from God were three things: true worship of God, love of neighbor, and hospitality to strangers. As the Israelites learned these three things, they would grow ready to challenge and change the world as it was, for the sake of the world that God intends. That was God's plan.

In the beginning, the children of Israel were not a nation but, rather, nomadic wanderers. Eventually, for economic reasons, they migrated to Egypt. At first they were welcomed by the Egyptians. Eventually, however, an atmosphere of anti-foreigner sentiment came to prevail in Egypt, and the detested Israelites were turned into slaves. God, however, through the leadership of Moses, led them out of slavery and, over the course of forty years of wilderness wanderings, guided them to a homeland of their own in the land of Canaan. There, they would learn life together in keeping with God's will for the world. Rather than being like the other nations, Israel would live with a knowledge of God and a commitment to God's ways that would set it apart from and even turn it into a light to the other nations. Israel would become a people through whom the rest of the world would meet with true knowledge of the God of liberating justice, compassionate righteousness, steadfast love, and merciful grace.

However, instead of becoming a light to the nations, Israel became just like the other nations. No sooner did the people begin settling into their new homeland than they started plotting the future they wanted for themselves, rather than serving the future intended by God. They started focusing on the prospect and pleasures of becoming a materially wealthy, politically prominent, and militarily mighty nation. Serving the same narrowly self-interested aims the other nations served, the Israelites took life into their own hands. Their worship of God became half-hearted and played second fiddle to worldly allurements and loyalties. They began accommodating themselves to the culture around them rather than challenging and changing it for God's sake. They began pledging to worldly rulers the kind of allegiance that should have been reserved for God alone. They began giving themselves over to expectations, customs, desires, and ways that ran counter to the aims and purposes of God. Their religious, political, and commercial leaders became self-serving and corrupt in their ways and oppressive toward the poor. Israel became a nation where, as Hosea, in another passage, puts it (4:1), "There is no faithfulness or loyalty, and no knowledge of God in the land."

What is God to do? That, for Hosea, is the question. And the passage we're reading this morning is about one route God could take. It's the route that can be heard in God's words, "I will now allure her [Israel], and bring her into the wilderness, and speak tenderly to her."

Luring Israel into the wilderness doesn't sound like a loving thing to do. The wilderness is desolate. In the wilderness, there is little to eat and drink, and there are no neighbors to extend a helping hand. The wilderness is filled with dangerous beasts. It is hovered over by death. In the wilderness, human life is marked by deep insecurity, anxiety, dread, and need.

Hosea, however, sought to remind his people of the good and important difference Israel's forty-year experience in the wilderness under the leadership of Moses had made. At no time in their history had the Israelites lived closer to God and more open to God's reality, truth, presence, and guidance than during that forty-year sojourn in the wilderness. In that wilderness, people couldn't fall back on their own strength, couldn't fall back on the worldly ways and means and customs and habits they ordinarily called on, to allay their fears and get what they wanted. In the wilderness, they were faced with overwhelming needs that they were powerless to meet without God's help. And, so, they leaned on God—they depended on God—as never before. They threw themselves open to God in a way they ordinarily would not have done. Precisely in the wilderness—precisely when confronted with the reality of wilderness insecurity, uncertainty, doubt, and anxiety beyond their power to do anything about it—the people lived closer to God than ever before. Precisely in the wilderness—distanced from the worldly ways and means and customs and habits they ordinarily leaned on to meet their desires and needs—they were most open to God and to God's word and will and way.

And in light of that fact, Hosea now declares to his people, "You are seeking your life and well-being through the ways and means and customs and habits you've taken on from the world around you, rather than through true worship of God, love of neighbor, and hospitality to strangers. You've closed yourselves off to knowledge of God. If there is again to be true knowledge of God in the land, and commitment to God's ways, perhaps it must come through a wilderness experience of being confronted with insecurity, uncertainty, doubt, and anxiety, beyond your power to do anything about it. Then you shall learn again as a people to move forward, guided not by self-serving ends and the expectations, customs, desires, and habits of the world around you, but by the word and will and way of God."

(2)

We, too, in oh-so many ways, tend to get caught up in seeking our life and well-being in a narrowly self-serving manner and through the ways and means and customs and habits of the world around us. We tend to minimize, neglect, or simply write off our need for God's nearness and for embracing the things that accord us with God's will, such as true worship of God, love of neighbor, and hospitality to strangers. We, too, accommodate ourselves to the expectations, customs, desires, and ways of the world in a manner that lets us forget that God actually intends for us to challenge and change the world for the sake of God's liberating justice, God's compassionate righteousness, God's steadfast love, and God's merciful grace. And sometimes what it takes to jar us loose from that and focus us anew on God is a wilderness experience.

Note well: that is not to say that God *makes* horrible things happen to people in order to make people turn to God. When we turn away from God's ways, God doesn't seek to win us back by employing divine terrorism. For God is out to win us to God's cause always and only through God's persuasive grace, love, mercy, and compassion. For example, God doesn't send plagues and illnesses to frighten us back to God; however, when plague or illness strikes, God *is* always there to help us draw forth something good from what is happening. God is with us and for us to ply us with the faith and hope and love and courage we need, for turning the sad and tragic circumstances we're in, into something that isn't merely sad and tragic—into something that actually makes the world *more* like rather than *less* like the world that God intends.

And the twofold fact of the matter is this. Fact #1: It is typical of us to become so caught up in our own self-serving ends and in accommodating ourselves to the expectations, customs, habits, and desires of the world around us that our worship of God becomes half-hearted at best. It is typical of us to seek our life and our well-being far more through the ways and means our culture encourages than by steeping ourselves in true knowledge of God in order rightly to challenge and change our culture. It is typical of us to so lose ourselves in the ways of the world around us that we fail even to be able to see anymore just how far from God's good aims and purposes we and our world have fallen. And Fact #2: More often than not, what is required to jar us loose from the hold the world has on us—what is required to refocus us on true worship of God—is a wilderness experience of our own. You see, such gains as success, victory, riches, comfort, happiness, and health tend to wed us more firmly to the world; they don't tend to intensify our desire for God and for a life of challenging and changing the world for God's sake. Strangely enough, perhaps, what actually is more likely to snatch us from the world's power over us and to open us most widely to God are failure, defeat, loss, shame, illness, death, suffering, crisis, tragedy, recognizing that we're in the gutter, realizing that our world is in chaos, being driven to confess that our life is out of control. It isn't *glorious* experiences but *wilderness* experiences that actually do the most to draw us toward God and the work of challenging and changing the world as it is, for the sake of the world that God intends.

(3)

Can we see the crisis called COVID-19 as a wilderness experience in Hosea's sense?

Surely the crisis we're in has all the trappings of such a wilderness experience. All around us, normal life has been knocked out of its sockets. We're being haunted by an invisible virus that has turned itself into a plague that is spreading widely and demonically across boundary after boundary and across precautionary barrier after precautionary barrier. Certain groups of people seem to be especially susceptible to attack, for example, the elderly and those with compromised immune systems or preexisting medical conditions. Yet the virus is dealing with victims somewhat unpredictably. Some it kills quickly; some it makes either slightly sick or deathly ill before letting go of them; some people barely notice—or don't notice at all!—that it's infected them and that they now are carrying the infection to others. To slow the virus's spread and to prevent it from overloading our health-care system to the point of crushing it, measures called "quarantining" and "social distancing" have been put into effect. These, in turn, have had their own way of disrupting lives. Many people who long and need to be together are being forced to stay apart. Others are being confined to tighter quarters together with each other than is healthy for anyone. Previously planned medical procedures and many newly arisen medical needs have been indefinitely put on hold. People needing treatment for addiction and other behavioral health issues aren't getting it. Great numbers of people are experiencing drastically reduced incomes. Schools have been closed. Public gatherings have been banned. Consumption of goods and services has evaporated. Unemployment has swept the land.

Rent and mortgage payments can't be made. Businesses have been closing down. Livelihoods are being wiped out. Hopes and dreams are dying. One nonprofit organization after the other has been brought to the brink of ruin. Political discourse is growing vitriolic and spiteful. And when public assistance is put on the table, power and greed grab quickly (and usually successfully) for the main course. And all this is happening with no clear end in sight. Even as our own state of Arkansas begins experimenting with measures aimed at restarting the economy while still protecting people's health, no one really knows where this is leading. No one really knows what the longer-term effect of this new coronavirus is going to be. It's hard to imagine the disruptive consequences of this plague just going away. The world feels strange and bizarre, even surreal. And we can't just clean the slate and start over. We find ourselves up against insecurity, uncertainty, doubt, and anxiety that we can't stop.

The question, though, is this: is the COVID-19 pandemic going to become for us a wilderness experience in the sense that Hosea means?

That it's a horrible experience goes without saying. But are we simply out to defeat this virus so that we can have life again the way we had it before? Or, while we seek to treat the sick and tend to the grieving, and while we seek a cure, and while we seek a vaccine, and while we work at minimizing societal harm, might we also let this experience throw us open to God in new ways? Might we let this experience open us to what is here to be learned about true worship of God, love of neighbor, and hospitality to strangers? Might we ask what God, amidst this horrible experience, might desire for us to learn about dwelling together in ways that challenge and change the world as it is, for the sake of the world intended by God's liberating justice, compassionate righteousness, steadfast love, and merciful grace? And what might that lesson be?

I said something here last Sunday that I want to bring up again today as one such lesson. What I said is this: you and I find ourselves haunted right now by a horrible experience. And yet, on any given day—on any given day prior to the outbreak of COVID-19, as still will be the case on any given day after this outbreak at last subsides—there are homes, there are neighborhoods, there are villages, cities, even countries, and sometimes regions of this world that have been turned into sites of horrifying and unrelenting hardship, calamity, disaster, sorrow, and suffering. And one thing I believe God would have us learn amidst the horrible experience we're caught up in right now is this: to never ever try to distance ourselves from the suffering of others, but to keep the suffering of others constantly, prayerfully on our hearts and minds, together with this question: what is ours to do this day, for the sake of God's love for the world? What is ours to do this day, not just to secure our own privileged place in the world, but for the sake of the world intended by God's liberating justice, compassionate righteousness, steadfast love, and merciful grace?

When God returned Jesus as the resurrected one to the world that crucified him, it was to bless the world with a new beginning—and to bless the followers of Jesus with the task of making that new beginning a meaningful reality for all God's children in every home, in every neighborhood, in every village, in every city, in every country, in every region of this world. It's an infinite task. We can't imagine accomplishing it in our own lifetime. But it's also an infinitely *good* task. And it's really what the time that God has given us on this Earth is finally all about. What matters in the end isn't striving for the world we want for ourselves, but serving the world that God intends for all God's children. Everywhere. In good times and in bad. Always. Amen.

11

Jeremiah 31:31–34 On the eve of destruction.

May 10, 2020, 5ᵗʰ Sunday of Easter

Greeting
The grace of the Lord Jesus Christ be with you all!

On the Christian worship calendar, we're in the season of Easter. In the Christian year, you see, "Easter" is more than just Easter Sunday. It refers also to a seven-week *season* of worship. And today is the fifth Sunday of the season of Easter.

The Easter season is intended especially as a time for becoming reminded of and reshaped in our identity as the community of Christ's resurrection Spirit.

Of course, right now, far fewer people in the United States are thinking about what today is on the Christian calendar than are thinking about what today is on the civic calendar of our country, where today is Mother's Day.

America's calendar of civic holidays plays a significant role in our lives. Its importance lies in how it keeps us mindful of people, events, and values that, in especially noteworthy ways, have given shape to the civil society and national entity that we have become.

The importance of the Christian worship calendar, on the other hand, is that it keeps us mindful of particular aspects of the life and mission of Jesus that need to shape what we, as his church, are becoming. It isn't commemorations focused on American social history, but commemorations focused on the history of Jesus Christ, that serve our growth in and as Christ's church.

That said, as we ready to worship God this fifth Sunday of Easter, I nevertheless would like to include a word regarding Mother's Day. I'd like in particular to offer a reminder of how Mother's Day began, at least as I have come to understand it.

Mother's Day became a national holiday in this country in 1914. That year, a congressional resolution established it for the sake of "a public expression of our love and reverence for the mothers of our country." This came about largely because of the efforts of a woman named Anna M. Jarvis. And *her* efforts grew out of the work of two other women, namely her own mother, an Appalachian homemaker and Sunday school teacher named Anna R. Jarvis, and a suffragist (an advocate for voting rights for women) from Boston named Julia Ward Howe, famously known as the author of "The Battle Hymn of the Republic."

The earliest Mother's Day was organized by Anna R. Jarvis in the mid-1800s. She called it "Mothers' Work Days." She focused on two things that she believed the men in her world were only superficially (if at all) concerned with, but that every community needed to become candidly and intensely concerned about, namely improved sanitation and health conditions for all and reconciliation between people whom the Civil War bitterly had divided.

About fifteen years later, Julia Ward Howe sought to have the day recognized as what she called a "Mother's Day for Peace." Howe earlier had not been a pacifist (indeed, she had written "The Battle Hymn of the Republic" in support of the military effort of the North in the Civil War). However, she became appalled at the carnage of the Civil War in America and of the Franco-Prussian War in Europe. One day, she was pondering the horrible tragedies of war, and she wrote this question on a piece of paper: "Why do not the mothers of mankind interfere in these matters, to prevent the waste of that human life of which they alone bear and know the cost?" And she issued an appeal to women everywhere to come together in common recognition of a Mother's Day for Peace.

When Mother's Day became an official American holiday in 1914, its focus was not identical with that of Howe and Jarvis in their concern for promoting society's common good and world peace. Mother's Day, as it is commemorated today, has become a somewhat different occasion than what was envisioned by its originators. It's now more focused on honoring mothers as such, and on recognizing and honoring the role played in our lives precisely by motherly care and devotion, motherly self-giving and even self-sacrifice, motherly grit and determination, motherly graciousness and affection, motherly backbone and resolve, and all the other things that go into what we try summing up with the term, *motherly love.*

And that is a good thing to do—an honorable thing, a respectful thing, a fitting thing to do. What I would add to that is simply this: in our celebration, we would do well to remember that the occasion does have its origin in three women's caring, gritty, gracious, determined, loving, and courageous insistence that we—as communities and as a society—need to stop being indifferent toward and, instead, need to become intensely concerned about tending to the well-being of all in our community and letting peace and love and understanding

get a real foothold and make a genuine difference in this world
that God so loves. Amen.

+ +

Announcements

I am Ruskin Falls. I serve as minister here. With me in our
sanctuary today are three other members of our church.
LaWanda Harris is serving as liturgist. Our music director, Sally
Todd, is at the piano. And our church sexton, David Harper, is
working the video end of things.

   New COVID-19 health-care guidelines are now in effect
in Arkansas regarding churches. The new directive strongly
encourages the use of "online worship platforms" only, rather
than returning too soon to in-person gatherings. However,
the directive does open the door to worshiping together in
person, *if* certain procedures are followed, such as avoiding all
physical contact and always keeping a considerable physical
distance from one another, wearing masks, eliminating the
passing around of offering plates or other items, refraining
from coming forward for communion or other purposes,
not offering childcare or youth classes, and keeping all areas
diligently sanitized.

   Our plan this week is to stick with what we've spent the
past six weeks learning how to do, namely, offering our service
of worship by way of a website video. The session of our church
will be meeting soon to decide on the timetable that makes the
most sense for our particular congregation to follow as events
unfold this week and in the weeks ahead. If you have thoughts
to share with us in this regard, please do that! And we'll keep

everyone well informed as to how we hope to proceed in the days and weeks ahead.

+ +

Jeremiah 31:31–34 *On the eve of destruction.*

TEXT *(English translation: NRSV)*

The days are surely coming, says the LORD, when I will make a new covenant with the house of Israel and the house of Judah. It will not be like the covenant that I made with their ancestors when I took them by the hand to bring them out of the land of Egypt—a covenant that they broke, though I was their husband, says the LORD. But this is the covenant that I will make with the house of Israel after those days, says the LORD: I will put my law within them, and I will write it on their hearts; and I will be their God, and they shall be my people. No longer shall they teach one another, or say to each other, "Know the LORD," for they shall all know me, from the least of them to the greatest, says the LORD; for I will forgive their iniquity, and remember their sin no more.

(1)

Jeremiah did not predict the coming of Jesus Christ. He didn't know how the new covenant was going to manifest itself in the world. He just declared what God had given him to proclaim amidst the horrifying events that had befallen his people at the hand of the armies of Babylon.

Those armies had overrun the homeland of the children of Israel. Jerusalem, the city the Israelites long had cherished as a sign of God's ongoing protection against enemy nations, lay in ruins. The king who sat on the royal throne of the house of David had been taken prisoner. The temple of the Lord had been turned to rubble and its contents either stolen or destroyed. Much of the surviving population was in the process of being driven into exile in a foreign land. All, it seemed, was lost. It was the darkest of times. Israel found itself on the eve of destruction. The faith of the children of Israel was in collapse.

This was the Israel through whom God, in the beginning, had set out to fill the world with true knowledge of God. Instructed by God's law, God's command, God's word, the people of Israel were intended by God to live together in a way that would turn them into a light to the nations. Israel's life together in the intimate embrace of God's own will was to light the way for all the world to learn the blessings of the compassion, mercy, loving kindness, justice, and peace of the God who had called Israel into being.

Yet, Israel failed its mission. Rather than becoming God's light to the other nations, Israel became just like the other nations. Competing with other nations for power and prestige on the world political stage, Israelite society became just as warped as all the others by forces of jealousy, greed, arrogance, injustice, violence, indifference, and lies.

And, just as other nations wax and wane, just as other nations come and go, so, now, Israel, too, had become a part of that historical process of rise and fall. And now Israel was on the eve of destruction.

There in the midst of precisely that darkness, there amidst his people's overwhelming sense of the absence of God, Jeremiah prophesied the coming of a time of light, a time of joy, a time when God would be recognized in a new and amazingly consoling, uplifting, and heartening way. The time is coming, he declared, when God shall join God's law, God's command, God's word, so intimately to the human heart that it is going to change how humanity knows God, and it is going to become a source of goodness and gladness for all the Earth.

In that day, declares Jeremiah, it will be given to all to hear in a new way the covenant promise God made of old to the children of Israel, that "I will be your God, and you shall be my people." In the day that is coming, it shall become clear that God's covenant promise doesn't mean, "Obey me or cease to be my people"; rather, it means, "I, your God, have, to all eternity, taken responsibility for your relationship with me. I will forgive all that needs forgiving; I will heal all that needs healing; I will redeem all that needs redeeming, in order to get you and your world where my love knows that you, in the end, most deeply need to be going."

Again: Jeremiah did not predict the life and mission of Jesus. Still, when we in the church celebrate Christ's life and mission, we are celebrating what Jeremiah prophesied. In Christ's life and mission, God reveals that God's covenant promise to Israel, and, through Israel, to all the world, boils down to this: God's determination to be with us and for us—God's determination never to be without us, never to be apart from us, but to be always at work in our lives to lift us into God's own life and guard us safe. In Jesus Christ God reveals God's law, God's command, God's word, not as a set of rules written on paper or carved in stone so that we can be condemned for breaking them, but as a person whose life and mission, whose words and deeds, whose birth and death and resurrection, imprint God's grace—imprint God's unconditional love—imprint God's free and unmerited forgiveness—on human hearts. You and I can break God's law, but we can't break God's grace! We can break God's commands, but we can't break God's unconditional love. We can break God's heart, but we can't break God's free forgiveness. The worst we can do is resist it, but that can't make God give up on us. And the most we can do is be grateful and glad, and then join the work of sharing this good news with all the world—which is to say, the work of the church. And that is the heart of what you and I are about, in and as Christ's church. For the church is about sharing, in word and deed—through what we proclaim and through what we do—through our way of being together and our way of serving others—the good news of Jesus Christ.

I like the incisive way in which theologian Karl Barth, at the end of his prolific teaching career, described the good news that is ours in the church to share with all the world.[7] The good news, Barth observed, is this: the God who is, is not a lonely God, infinitely far away, majestically and self-sufficiently detached from all that isn't God; God is not a divinity who has inhumanly or superhumanly set itself apart from humanity and now relates to us only in terms of impersonal laws and legalistic commands. Rather, God is God only as *Immanuel*—God is

---

[7] Karl Barth, *Evangelical Theology: An Introduction,* trans. Grover Foley (Grand Rapids: William B. Eerdmans, 1963), 10–11.

God only as the God who is determined to all eternity to be with us and for us in our humanity as the bringer of help and healing and peace and joy and courage beyond anything the world itself could ever give. God exists neither next to us nor merely beyond us, but, rather, always with us, by us, and, most importantly, for us in the humanity of Jesus. In coming among us in this way in the humanity of Jesus, God reveals that God's deity includes humanity, and that God always meets us where and as we are, in the midst of both our highest hopes and our hardest fears, to guide and direct us in our own strivings and struggles to become human in a world that's filled to the brim with inhumane darkness.

You see, in coming among us in this way—in coming among us in the life and mission of the Jesus Christ whose own path was marked by so much human suffering and yet who was so profoundly set on giving of himself for the good of others—in coming among us in this way, God opens up a new and amazing place in the human heart. God opens up a place where we know that—independently of all holy cities, thrones, temples, and other shrines, and even when the darkness is so great that all outward signs of God's presence and protection seem to have vanished—whatever else our lives may mean, we were put here on this Earth to love and to be loved, and this love that we belong to shall never die, shall never give up on us.

That is what we, in and as Christ's church, are called to be about: sharing the good news of Jesus Christ with all the world. That sharing includes serving what our Presbyterian Church (U.S.A.) *Book of Order* calls "The Great Ends of the Church," which are these (F-1.0304): the proclamation of the gospel for the salvation of humankind; the shelter, nurture, and spiritual fellowship of the children of God; the maintenance of divine worship; the preservation of the truth; the promotion of social righteousness; and the exhibition of the Kingdom of Heaven to the world.

As we put it in our own church's visitor brochure: *Jesus* is the founder of the church, whose gospel has grasped our lives as the very word of God, comforting, challenging, and directing us, like nothing in this world, in redeeming ways. The *church* is a way of being together, organized to bring the gospel of Jesus to bear on all of life, for the sake of the future that God is calling into being and calling us to serve. *Redemption* is the event of God's loving embrace, fitting us for a better tomorrow by transforming human ambiguity, anxiety, resentment, and fear into a faith, hope, love, and courage that liberate us from destructive and self-destructive ways. And *service* is a prayerfully considered response to Jesus's call to us to love God with all our heart, soul, mind, and strength, and to love our neighbors as ourselves.

As the apostle Paul has noted (Romans 12:2), our task as Christ's church is to live not conformed to our world, but transformed by the good news Christ came bringing—and this for the good of all the world. And the world does deeply need what is ours to do.

(2)

There is, however, this problem: like Israel in Jeremiah's day, the church today, at least in North America, is on the eve of destruction.

The church finds itself today in a world marked by radically declining interest in the church and, as a result, by a radical decline in church membership, in the amount of financial support the church receives, and in the extent of people's participation in its services of worship and other activities. The simple—and sociologically measurable—fact is this: ever increasingly, the world that we now live in wants no truck with the church, wants no dealings with the church, indeed feels alienated from the church and all its talk of God's word sounding forth through biblical testimony to a first-century Palestinian Jew named Jesus. Our own society increasingly regards the church as a waste of time and money, an indulgence in fantasy and illusion, and an obstacle to the good life. At a rapid pace, our world is growing estranged from the church and what the church calls *proclamation of the word of God*. And this situation has drawn the church into what would seem to be a time of decline—indeed, a time that has the potential to undo the church altogether.

None of that, however, is what is destroying the church. What is destroying the church is a force at work within the church. It is the force of fear. Fearful of growing smaller, poorer, and more marginal in American society, churches are trying to pull in new members and money by making themselves more attractive to the world. Increasingly, churches look around to see what now interests, what attracts, what titillates, what excites people in the world outside the church, and then they try replicating those things inside the church. They try to make themselves equally interesting, attractive, titillating, and exciting, so that folks who otherwise wouldn't now will come and stay and give. As Jeremiah saw ancient Israel failing its mission by trying to be just like rather than God's light to the other nations, so the church perhaps is failing its mission by trying to be just like rather than God's light to the world it's in. But, of course, this is not a new temptation! The church always has existed in the tension created by the fact that we humans can't help but be in and of the world, whereas the church's calling is to be in and for but not simply of the world.

Christ did not create the church to be like the world around it. Nor did he create the church to be a way of withdrawing from the world. Rather, he created the church to be how and where his resurrection Spirit shall enable people faithfully, creatively, humbly, boldly, passionately, compassionately, gladly, graciously, and thoughtfully to dwell in the tension between the world as it is and the very different world that God intends. Christ created the church to be how and where his resurrection Spirit shall enable people to reflect into our world of jealousy, greed, arrogance, injustice, violence, indifference, and lies, the amazingly consoling, uplifting, heartening, and world-changing compassion, mercy, loving-kindness, justice, and peace of the creator of all things, who is determined to all eternity to be with us and for us in our humanity as the bringer of help and healing and peace and joy and courage beyond anything the world itself could ever give.

Perhaps the real problem today is that the church has grown so comfortable in the world as it is that we've become unable to hear God's word judging us, redeeming us, and thereby challenging us to move away from our comfort zones and to learn to swim against the stream and cut against the grain of the present order of things. Perhaps the real problem today is that the church has become so self-satisfied that it actually has forgotten and, in effect, begun turning away from the tasks and responsibilities that go with being the community of the hearers and doers of God's word—which tasks and responsibilities, by the way, can't be learned from the world but only from God's word itself! Or do we even know what we're talking about anymore when we talk about "the word of God"? Have we perhaps lost touch with—are we in need of learning anew—what it means to hear and heed God's word? Might it be that the present situation of the church is precisely not a call to accommodate our message to the world, but, rather, a call to reformation in the church grounded in a new hearing of God's word? Might it be that our great need right now is this: for Christ's sake, to become more daring!?

Amen.

12

Hebrews 1:1–3a; 4:12–13   How the light gets in.

May 17, 2020, 6th Sunday of Easter

Greeting
The grace of the Lord Jesus Christ be with you all!

On the calendar of the Christian year, we're in what the church calls Eastertide, the season of Easter. Easter is a seven-week season of worship intended especially to help us be reminded of and reshaped in our identity as God's resurrection people—and this, so that, day by day, we may grow in readiness to hear, to proclaim, and to show the gospel of Jesus Christ our Lord.

It belongs to my prayer that this service of worship shall help us all to become more clearly, more dearly, and more nearly attuned to the mystery and goodness of God, and to the courage that God desires for us to have and to inspire in others. Amen.

+ +

Announcements
For the sake of visitors, let me say that I am Ruskin Falls. I serve as minister for this congregation. With me in our sanctuary today are four other members of our church. LaWanda Harris is serving as liturgist. Our music director, Sally Todd, is at the piano, and also will be playing the organ. (We believe, at any

rate, that we have the organ in working shape today!) Choir member Ferris Allen will lead in singing. And our church sexton, David Harper, is working the video end of things.

As I expect you know, Arkansas (among other states) now is trying to move away from the degree of social distancing we have been practicing and to move into more of a normalizing of social contact around the state. Indeed, new health and safety guidelines are now in place in Arkansas that allow for in-person services of worship in Arkansas churches, provided certain important measures are adhered to. Officials still are encouraging churches, for the time being, to stick to online platforms only, rather than gathering in person in their buildings. However, allowance is being made for individual churches to decide for themselves how to proceed at this point. Our church session will be meeting this afternoon (not face-to-face, but rather by Zoom), and we will be discussing, among other things, what makes the most sense for our congregation right now, with respect to either opening up our building for in-person services or continuing for now with online worship. We will be getting word out to everyone regarding where that discussion leads and how we plan to proceed.

We still don't know just what course the new coronavirus is going to take—and take us on. I think it is fair to say that there's still going to be a lot of sickness; there will be more deaths; and, even best-case scenario, there's going to be a whole lot of continued suffering from the financial hardships that have been imposed on people due to the measures that need to be taken in the face of the health risks this virus poses. There's simply not a solution to our viral situation that won't bring with it lots of pain and suffering. As individuals and as a society, we're up against a still-hard test of our moral courage, our societal compassion, our political goodwill, and our social and scientific wisdom. And in any case, we need to remember that we are not seeking what is *good* if it isn't the *common* good we seek.

+ +

Hebrews 1:1–3a; 4:12–13   *How the light gets in.*

TEXT *(English translation: NRSV)*

> Long ago God spoke to our ancestors in many and various ways by the prophets, but in these last days he has spoken to us by a Son, whom he appointed heir of all things, through whom he also created the worlds. He is the reflection of God's glory and the exact imprint of God's very being, and he sustains all things by his powerful word.
>
> Indeed, the word of God is living and active, sharper than any two-edged sword, piercing until it divides soul from spirit, joints from marrow; it is able to judge the thoughts and intentions of the heart. And before him no creature is hidden, but all are naked and laid bare to the eyes of the one to whom we must render an account.

(1)

The word of God is living and active. It doesn't passively wait for us to chance across it. Rather, God's word comes toward us, it comes at us, it confronts and challenges us. It strips us naked and lays us bare before God's judgment. It brings our view of ourselves, our world, and God, face-to-face with what God has to say to us regarding ourselves, our world, and God.

Some two thousand years ago, the living and active word of God looked out upon humanity through the eyes of Jesus, addressed humanity through the voice of Jesus, and touched humanity through the hand of Jesus. God's word actively revealed itself through Jesus. Through him it captured and commanded human hearts and minds, drawing disciples to move beyond this world's ways of categorizing and treating them, to become instead who they are in God's eyes. At first, even Jesus's closest disciples had a hard time understanding his life and mission. However, particularly through his presence as the crucified yet resurrected one, they came to understand themselves as having been graciously and lovingly laid bare before the judgment seat of God. They found themselves, at one and the same time, confronted with the waywardness of their lives up to that point and turned into recipients of unimaginably loving guidance from God. Through the living presence of Jesus, God's word exposed his followers to their presently ungodly ways—their sin—and to God's unconditional love for them.

We today don't have the company of Jesus the way they did. We don't have direct access to his living eyes, his living voice, his living touch. What we have instead is the community of his Holy Spirit and the wisdom and traditions this community passes down to us from those who did walk with Jesus. What we have is their witness to Jesus; we have the effect that his eyes, his voice, his touch, had on them. This is the witness that comes to us through the words of scripture that we call the Bible. We have the Old Testament witness that anticipates his coming, and we have the New Testament witness that recollects his having come. These, together, bear witness to the living word of God that looked out through the eyes of Jesus, that spoke out through the voice of Jesus, and that reached out through the hand of Jesus. The words of the Bible bear witness to Jesus as the living word of God who actively strips us naked before God's judgment by laying us bare before God's unconditional love.

Note well: the words of the Bible are not God's word. Rather, they witness uniquely *to* God's word. They are human words that have come about through prophetic and apostolic witness to the living and active word of God at work in the history of Jesus Christ, which includes God's creation of the people of Israel, and the life and mission of Jesus that grew from that. Indeed, the words of the Bible are the witness to Jesus Christ through which his resurrection Spirit confronts us in the church today with God's word. The Spirit uses the life of the church to create in us eyes and ears for God's word coming at us through these words of scripture. The work of the Spirit turns encounter with the Bible into encounter with Jesus, interrupting, addressing, and commanding us as God's own word, opening us to God's creative aim and purposes, and conforming us to God's good will and way. Through the Bible we look to Jesus and find ourselves grasped by God's own word.

We can't say just how the Spirit uses the church to accomplish that. We can't explain, in natural cause-and-effect terms, the gift of eyes and ears for God's word coming at us through the witness of scripture. What we can do, though, is testify to our encounter with God's word through that witness; what we can do is testify to its living and active presence among us, giving us new and different, indeed, divine, direction.

(2)

How can we know when it isn't just human words but God's word that we are hearing? I believe a good starting place is this morning's passage from the book of Hebrews.

If it is God's word coming at us and not just human words, then it will leave us naked and laid bare before God's judgment on our life. It will actively challenge us, piercing our depths, cutting through all the errors, lies, and self-deceptions that are there. It will confront our view of ourselves and our world with God's view. It will judge us as only the God revealed in Jesus Christ can judge us. It will be a word that uncovers all our sin, all our ways of walling God out, all our ways of living for ourselves apart from God, all our ways of justifying ourselves when we're actually only trying to avoid or hide from God. And it will do all that not to condemn us but to save us. It will leave us naked and laid bare not to doom and punish us, but to lavish on us God's free grace, God's infinite mercy, God's eternal forgiveness, God's unconditional love. If it is God's word coming at us, it won't be a purely punishing word, nor will it be a word that just leaves us as we were. Rather, it will be a word that judges us as only God can judge. It will be a word that judges us with unconditional love. It will declare to us our sin while simultaneously declaring to us God's promise that sin's power to ruin us shall never exceed God's power to redeem us. If all you hear is, "You're bad!" that wasn't God's word. If all you hear is, "You're good!" or even "You're OK!" that wasn't God's word. God's word is this: "You are avoiding and evading me! You're resisting my will and way! You have turned the world into and tolerated it as a world of sin! Nevertheless, I love you unconditionally. There's a place and role for you in the future that I am calling into being, and my love shall take you there!"

(3)

My job as preacher is to proclaim to you God's word.

There are many things that, though widely associated with preaching, are not the same as proclaiming God's word. There are things that, though often associated with preaching, nevertheless are not what I, as preacher, am here for. For example, I'm not here to entertain you or to display my oratorical skills (or lack thereof!). I'm not here to teach you life principles that can make you a happier, healthier, or more prosperous individual. I'm not here to give personal advice on how to advance your career or improve your relationships or have a winning personality or be a good citizen. I'm not here to win you over to a particular school of thought. I'm not here to make you feel good about yourself, nor am I here to make you feel bad about yourself. I'm not here to tell you how to vote or what political party to side with. I'm not even here to tell you where you must stand on the issues of the day, and I'm certainly not here to fan your emotions regarding those issues. I'm not here to get you to think and act as I do, or as I happen to believe a "good Presbyterian" should, or even as I happen to believe a "good Christian" does. I'm not here to tell you what to think, feel, believe, or do in your own daily life, and I'm not here to add my commentary to what's already out there on all the hot topics of the social media moment. I'm not even here to try to be relevant to any of that.

To be sure, I may have pertinent things to say regarding such matters. In any given sermon, I might be heard advocating a particular political view, moral stance, or personal course of action. After all, God's word *is* about God's giving and our receiving guidance and direction, including political, moral, and personal guidance and direction. Still, it is important to remember that preaching is not about me winning you over to my take on the issues of the day. Preaching is not about my knowing and telling you just what your take on such things should be.

For starters, there are many things that I can't know about what God is up to in your life. God may be working with you in ways that I can't even imagine. The things that God is up to in your life are unique to God's relationship with *you*. The guidance and direction that God gives to us is not a one-size-fits-all sort of gift. Each of us is a unique individual with our own strengths and our own ways of using and of squandering those strengths—and with our own weaknesses and our own ways of overcoming and of yielding to those weaknesses. Therefore, God does not work with us identically but with us as unique individuals who are pushed and pulled along by our own unique cultural, social, psychological, spiritual, and biological makeup. What God expects *me* to think, feel, say, and do in a given situation may not be identical with what God expects *you* to think, feel, say and do in a similar situation. I may sometimes have sound insight into what God actually is urging you to think, feel, say, and do. Still, I can't be certain. And it's not my job as preacher to presume or pretend to be certain.

There are many things that are widely associated with preaching and some that even are inevitable accompaniments of preaching, that nevertheless are not what my job as preacher is about. My job as preacher is to proclaim to you God's word.

My job is to proclaim here and now the word of God that has spoken and speaks itself into the world through Jesus Christ and the biblical witness to his life and mission. My job is to do my best to listen for God's word coming at us through the history of Jesus Christ and then to say what I hear in ways that help you hear for yourself what God is speaking into your heart and mind and life right now. My job is to listen prayerfully closely, and, then, in our gathered presence, to let my striving to hear God's word give impetus to your striving to hear God's word for yourself.

We're not together right now to give my words a hearing. Nor are we here simply to give the words of the Bible a hearing. We're here to lean into Christ's Holy Spirit and pray that, as the biblical witness to God's word is proclaimed in the preacher's oh-so human words, the very word of God shall reveal itself. We're here to lean into the Holy Spirit and, hopefully and expectantly, to pray for God to give us to know what we can't know without God's help, namely God's reality, will, and way—who God is and what God is up to in our lives—why we're here and what God expects of us—and what God has done and is doing to weave us into the greater fabric of the future that God intends.

We're not here for the sake of political, moral, or personal counsel from me regarding my take on the issues of the day. We're here to be kept mindful of the following three things: that God abides in utter mystery, unobservable, unmeasurable, ungraspable, unimaginable, unknowable from any merely human point of view; that, through the life and mission of Jesus Christ and the biblical witness to his history, God nevertheless has and does act to communicate to us God's reality, will, and way; and that we have the promise of the Holy Spirit to turn the church's proclamation of God's word into God's way of speaking guidance and direction into each of our lives amidst whatever cultural, social, psychological, spiritual, and biological forces are pushing and pulling on us.

(4)

And one time more: what is the sign that it is God's word that you are hearing?

When it's God's word, it strips you naked and lays you bare before the judgment seat of God's love. When it's God's word, it lets you see, in your view of yourself and of your world, errors, lies, and self-deceptions that need to be confronted and changed by God's very different view of you and of your world. When it's God's word, it calls you into question; it interrogates and challenges your thoughts and feelings about God, about others, and about yourself—the way the living presence of Jesus interrogated and challenged followers two thousand years ago. When it's God's word, it strips you naked and lays you bare so that you may see yourself as God judges you, and others as God judges them, thus releasing you from your presently false judgment of yourself and of others. When it's God's word, it confronts you as no mere human can with the great mystery of sin—the great mystery that we actually prefer clothing ourselves in errors, lies, and self-deceptions, rather than seeing ourselves and others as God does—even though what God sees in us all is this: children of God's unconditional love!

When God strips us naked and lays us bare, what God sees are beings who are terribly flawed, cunningly selfish, amazingly self-contradictory, incredibly unfaithful to God, deeply unprepared to trust the lordship of Jesus, and yet, nevertheless, at the same time, beings who are the object of God's compassion, mercy, and forgiveness—beings whom God desires to love into changing; beings whom God desires to change into more loving beings, by graciously conforming us to God's living and active word.

Still, though, even knowing all that, something in us still resists letting God pierce our depths too thoroughly with God's word. Something in us resists letting ourselves become changed too radically by God. Again: that is the mystery of sin. Sin actually armors us against and walls us off from the love that gave us life and that awaits us at life's end.

We in the church, however, are blessed to know and live by this promise from God: where scripture's witness to Jesus Christ is soundly proclaimed and heard, the Holy Spirit will be there, working to open us to God's word, even if the Spirit accomplishes this just a little at a time—even if the Spirit accomplishes this only ever so slowly, by making little cracks here and there in the armor and the walls of our resistance to God's word. That's—if I may borrow a line from Leonard Cohen's song, "Anthem"—*how the light gets in*. Through the life of the church, the Holy Spirit works on us, making little cracks here and there in the armor and the walls of our sinful self, to let shine into our hearts and minds and lives the light of God's living word of guidance, grace, and love.

Blessed are those God's word has cracked, even if only a little, for that's how the light gets in.

Amen.

13

1ˢᵗ Peter 3:13–18a By gracious powers.

May 24, 2020, 7ᵗʰ Sunday of Easter

Greeting

The grace of the Lord Jesus Christ be with you all!

On the worship calendar of the church, today is the seventh and final Sunday of Eastertide. Easter is the day each year when we in the church commemorate Jesus's return, as the resurrected one, to the world that crucified him. Easter also is a forty-nine-day *season* of worship, intended as a time for taking to heart this truth: to be blessed with nearness to the resurrected Jesus is to be blessed also with a task—the task of learning to let our lives, "more clearly, more dearly, and more nearly," revere and honor what God has done and does for the world through the history of Jesus Christ.

It belongs to my prayer that God shall bless us now with a glad and reverent sense of God's presence among us, lifting hearts, stretching minds, and moving wills to help us become the Easter people we are called and blessed to be. Amen.

+ +

Announcements

I am Ruskin Falls. I serve as minister for this congregation. With me in our sanctuary today are four other members of

139

our church. Church sexton David Harper is doing the video recording. Music director Sally Todd is at the piano and also will be at the organ. Choir member Mary Kai Clark is our soloist and song leader today. And LaWanda Harris is our liturgist.

Let me note that I will be away from the pulpit next Sunday, May 31, and LaWanda will be doing the preaching that day. For newcomers to our online services, let me note that LaWanda is a nurse here in Little Rock, working at Arkansas Hospice. She also is in the third of four years of seminary studies, working on her Master of Divinity degree in the distance program of the University of Dubuque Theological Seminary. And she has been a good shoulder for me to be able to lean on these past weeks, as I have gone about learning to lead worship in front of a camera. This is not something I was ever cut out to do, and LaWanda has been great at helping me smile my way through it. I very much look forward to having LaWanda fill this pulpit next Sunday in my stead! Then I'll be back at it on June 7.

We are, of course, providing online worship services because of the health concerns brought about by the outbreak of COVID-19. While officials still are encouraging the continuation of online-only platforms for worship, at this point, churches are permitted to conduct in-person services, so long as they adhere to certain clear and important guidelines. The session of our church has decided to continue with online worship only, through at least June 14, after which we will review the advisability of reopening the church for in-person services of worship and our readiness to do that in keeping with good health-care guidelines.

In the meantime, I do pray that this, our humble effort at going online in order to keep worship at the center of our congregational life, is proving helpful. Let me say also this: if these video services have been your introduction to the life of our church, I invite you, when our church reopens, and when you personally begin feeling OK again about being around groups, to come by one Sunday and join us in person. I will add that we easily are able to do a lot of physical distancing. Our sanctuary was built back in the 1950s, when the membership of this church was ten times what it is today. We presently don't fill this room with people, but we have plenty of room for spreading out. What we do fill this room with is lots of warmth, lots of loving affection, and lots of desire for truth and for doing God's goodness justice. So, I invite you to consider joining us here for worship one day, be it only occasionally or be it regularly. We look forward to greeting and meeting you face-to-face.

+ +

1st Peter 3:13–18a   *By gracious powers.*

TEXT *(English translation: NRSV)*

Now who will harm you if you are eager to do what is good? But even if you do suffer for doing what is right, you are blessed. Do not fear what they fear, and do not be intimidated, but in your hearts sanctify Christ as Lord. Always be ready to make your defense to anyone who demands from you an accounting for the hope that is in you; yet do it with gentleness and reverence. Keep your conscience clear, so that, when you are maligned, those who abuse you for your good conduct in Christ may be put to shame. For it is better to suffer

for doing good, if suffering should be God's will, than
to suffer for doing evil. For Christ also suffered for sins
once for all, the righteous for the unrighteous, in order
to bring you to God.

(1)

The letter we call 1ˢᵗ Peter was written during a time when there
was widespread prejudice against Christians. It was written
during a time when mainstream culture tended to look down
on Christians as persons filled with outlandish yet troubling
notions regarding an executed criminal named Jesus—notions
that made Christians sound and seem disloyal to the Roman
Empire, contemptuous of Roman religion and its deities, and
undesirable to have around as family, friends, neighbors, or
fellow workers. It was a time when the decision to become
a Christian, the decision to follow Jesus as a member of his
church, could, at any minute, in some way or another, become
costly. Christians had to reckon with the possibility that they
might be made to suffer for that decision. In chapter four, it is
put this way (verses 12–13):

> Beloved, do not be surprised at the fiery ordeal that is
> taking place among you to test you, as though some-
> thing strange were happening to you. But rejoice insofar
> as you are sharing Christ's suffering, so that you may
> also be glad and shout for joy when his glory is revealed.

People will, of course, be skeptical of Christian gladness and
joy. Therefore, as we just read, "Be ready to make your defense

to anyone who demands from you an accounting for the *hope* that is in you."

(2)

I would like for us this morning to consider the matter of Christian hope. And I want to move in that direction with a few words regarding the hymn that Mary Kai will be singing immediately following this sermon. The hymn is "By Gracious Powers."[8] The text was written by Dietrich Bonhoeffer in December 1944. Bonhoeffer was a Lutheran minister and theologian in Germany. In 1944, Germany was waging war against the world. A decade earlier, in 1933, Adolf Hitler and his Nazi movement had risen to power in Germany. At that time, German society was heavily impacted by a severe economic crisis, a widespread feeling of disgrace over their defeat in the last war, violent social turmoil, bitter political division, and heightened fear throughout their land. In that atmosphere, many Germans had become convinced that their nation needed the authoritarian and nationalistic arm of a strong leader such as Hitler to get them back on their feet, to restore their historical pride, and to secure their future. They believed in Hitler and his vision for pulling Germany out of its present condition of weakness and disgrace and returning their country to the values and greatness of a past when Germany had been a proud empire. Even most Christians believed that God was on Hitler's side. The overwhelming majority of Christians in Germany

---

[8] In *Glory to God: A Presbyterian Hymnal* (Louisville: Westminster John Knox Press, 2013), #818.

were supportive of Hitler and of letting the church become assimilated into the Nazi political orientation, even when that orientation called for brutal discrimination against Jews and other despised groups, and even when that orientation, in 1939, sparked World War II.

Bonhoeffer publicly and adamantly opposed Hitler and the Nazi ideology from the start. And, when war broke out, his opposition took an important turn: his anti-Nazi resistance got him involved in secret plots to help Jews escape Nazi brutalities and also in a secret plot to put an end to Adolf Hitler and Nazi rule once and for all. However, in 1943, Bonhoeffer's involvement in the resistance movement was uncovered by Nazi authorities. He was imprisoned while authorities sought to uncover the details regarding the membership and activities of the resistance movement he was in. When, from his prison cell in December 1944, Bonhoeffer wrote "By Gracious Powers," he knew that he was subject to being executed at any time. That time came on April 9, 1945, when, by order of Hitler himself, Bonhoeffer was stripped naked, led to the prison gallows, and hanged. He was thirty-nine years old.

When, in a moment, Mary Kai sings "By Gracious Powers," I urge you to pay close attention to the words, and to keep in mind the conditions under which Bonhoeffer wrote them. He was prayerfully persuaded that, in order to follow Jesus and the way of the cross, he had to resist Nazism, challenge Hitler's power, fight against the Nazification of the church, and work to save Jews from the forces of antisemitism despite whatever suffering it might bring him, and even should it cost him his life. And, in the midst of all the suffering he endured, he wrote—and I would also say he believed and lived—these words:

> *By gracious powers so wonderfully sheltered,*
> *and confidently waiting, come what may,*
> *we know that God is with us night and morning,*
> *and never fails to greet us each new day.*

That, it seems to me, is a wonderful expression of Christian hope. It's a wonderful expression of the kind of hope that is at the heart of the New Testament letter of 1st Peter. This is hope that is grounded in recognition that God is present amidst all the powers of evil and suffering and death in this world, to redeem us from those powers. This is hope that is grounded in recognition that God is with us and for us to give our lives meaning and direction even when our cup is, as Bonhoeffer writes, "filled to brimming with bitter suffering, hard to understand."

(3)

Critics of Christianity tend to equate Christian hope with wishful thinking. While the hope we have actually derives from the experience of God's redeeming presence in the world, critics charge that we believe in God merely because, in the face of evil, suffering, and death, we wish for the kind of security that only such a God could give.

We Christians need to be clear that there is a deep difference between hope that is Christian and hope that is merely wishful.

The theologian Charlotte Martin, in her book, *Dynamics of Hope,* is helpful here, with the distinction she makes between true hope and mere wishfulness.[9] As an illustration, she invites us to imagine two students going into a classroom to take an exam, each thinking to themself, "I sure hope I get a decent grade on this test." However, the first student thinks that to himself, knowing that he didn't study for the exam, and knowing that he got a fairly low grade on an earlier exam in that class, even though he did study for it. The second student, on the other hand, is going into the exam having studied for it for a long time, and having the feeling that, for the large part, she understood the material. Under those circumstances, the first student's hope sounds like this: "I sure hope I come out OK, even though I didn't get to study, and even though I barely passed the first test, which I did study for." And the second student's hope sounds like this: "I believe I can do all right since I studied hard and most of the material made sense." This second student's hope has a firm connection to something *real*. She is aware of something in the present—namely, her preparedness—that gives her hope an element of reasoned expectation. She has good reason to envision her present situation moving toward the desired outcome. On the other hand, the first student's wish for a decent grade lacks similar contact with anything in the present that gives good reason to envision his situation moving toward the outcome he desires.

Mere wishfulness isn't based in reality. In a way, it even denies reality. It gives the imagination free rein. I can wish for a good test score, even though the reality is that I'm totally unprepared. Mere wishfulness doesn't have to bother with the

---

[9] Charlotte Joy Martin, *Dynamics of Hope: Eternal Life and Daily Christian Living* (Collegeville, MN: The Liturgical Press, 2002), 11ff.

facts. I can wish for whatever I choose, even if there's no genuine reason to expect it as an outcome.

True hope, on the other hand, as Charlotte Martin puts it, "keeps faith with reality".[10] "Wishing can occur in any situation at all;" true hope, on the other hand, "can occur only sometimes".[11] True hope can occur only when we are in touch with a condition or power in the present that we have reason to expect to bring about the desired outcome. I can't truly hope for just anything. I can have true hope only when I'm in touch with something real that gives me reason to expect the present to lead to the desired future.

(4)

Christian hope has a firm connection to something real, namely, the history of Jesus Christ. The scriptures, preaching, sacraments, and fellowship of the church that Christ called into being connect us to his life, his mission, his word, his Holy Spirit. They connect us to the power of his gospel to heal broken lives, make the weak strong, and revive the afflicted; they connect us to his power to give direction to the lost, bravery to the lowly, humility to the proud, generosity to the selfish, love to the loveless, dignity to the belittled and the shamed, joy to those carrying heavy burdens, and freedom to those fettered by unmerciful forces. Through the church, you and I are joined to the power of the gospel of Jesus to give us new eyes and ears for the presence and power of eternal God in the world—not a God of wishful thinking, not a God who serves our whims, not

[10] Ibid., 19
[11] Ibid., 24.

a God connected to nothing beyond our desires and fears, but rather the God who demands to be known through the cross and resurrection of Jesus—the God who judges and redeems through the love that looks out at us through Jesus when he declares, "Neither sin nor suffering nor death shall have the final word over your life. God is fitting you for a place and role in God's coming kingdom. And that kingdom is at hand! Repent and believe in the gospel. And come, follow me."

Through the history of Jesus Christ, through his gospel, through his life and mission, through his crucifixion and resurrection, we have been drawn into God's own life and opened to the promise of God's redeeming grace—God's promise to love us unconditionally and forever. Through communion with Jesus, we receive new eyes and ears for the reality, truth, and presence of the God who *is* the true hope of the world. And the more we give ourselves over to learning Christ's life and mission—the more we give ourselves over to following the way of his cross in the light of his resurrection—the more genuinely hope-filled our lives actually become, whatever our circumstances.

And do note the order of things here. Christian hope is not the result of certain things we tell ourselves regarding Jesus. Rather, our beliefs regarding Jesus express the hope that has been given us through our experience of the redeeming work of his Spirit among us. Our hope is grounded in the relationship that Jesus has created with us. It is grounded in the new eyes and ears his Spirit gives us.

(5)

It is because we have this hope, 1st Peter reminds us, that we need not fear as others fear. We need not fear the powers of evil, suffering, and death. We need not become intimidated by the troubles, woes, worries, and sorrows that we experience in this world. Indeed, another word for Christian hope precisely is *courage*. Christian hope is part and parcel of the courage created in and among us through Christ's resurrection Spirit. It goes hand in glove with the courage the Holy Spirit plies us with to follow Jesus and strive to do God's goodness justice in all circumstances, no matter what, and come what may.

Fear diminishes life. When fearful people are powerless, their fear robs them of the ability to thrive and flourish—and it robs them, too, of their ability to help others thrive and flourish. And when fearful people are powerful, their fear makes them selfish, greedy, cynical, and cruel. It leaves them so narrowly focused on their own private interests that they never really learn or get taken up into the kind of love for others that God created us to know, enjoy, and share—the kind of love in which life that really and truly thrives and flourishes is always rooted.

On the other hand, the courage that is ours through Jesus Christ adds wonder, joy, beauty, and cheerful promise to life, whatever our circumstances. For Christian courage is the event of eternal God speaking into our hearts and minds and lives the compassionate love, redemptive healing, and gracious transformation that God is calling us to serve for the sake of the world that God's graciously redeeming love intends.

God is, in God's own mysterious way, working changes in this world. And some of those changes God is out to bring about specifically in and through you and me. God has work for us to do. God has tasks for us to take up. And, in the present world, what God is calling us to do will sometimes turn out to be challenging, even risky, even intimidating, even dangerous.

However, what God is calling us to do is and always will be
something aimed at readying us and others for the amazing
future that Jesus called God's coming kingdom.

As Dietrich Bonhoeffer wrote from that Nazi prison cell in
1944, no matter how dire the present, we can trust the future
that God is calling into being. And because we can trust that
future, we also can expect that, whatever God is calling us to do
and in whatever circumstances, we will be wonderfully sheltered
by gracious powers that free us from fear; gracious powers
that lift us into life that is genuinely joyful, compassionately
courageous, and ever filled with true hope; gracious powers
whose hold on us lets us genuinely, compassionately, and really
and truly hope-filled, thrive and flourish in this world, no
matter what, and come what may. Amen.

(14)

2nd Corinthians 13:11–13   Holy kiss, triune God, and peace.

June 7, 2020, Trinity Sunday

Greeting
The grace of the Lord Jesus Christ be with you all!

On the worship calendar of the church, today is Trinity Sunday. Our civic calendar is designed to orient us toward significant aspects of the past that have made us the civil society and the national entity that we are. The worship calendar of the church, on the other hand, is designed to orient us toward significant aspects of the life and mission of Jesus Christ. The most widely commemorated Christian calendar events are Christmas, Easter, and Pentecost. Like them, Trinity Sunday is intended to be a worship occasion that helps to draw us into the history and Spirit of Jesus. There is, though, this difference: while the other occasions are focused on a specific event, such as the birth of Jesus or his crucifixion and resurrection or the birth of the church through the Holy Spirit, the focus of Trinity Sunday is not so much on a particular act of God, as it is on the unfathomable mystery of God's being as the Trinity of Creator, Redeemer, Comforter—or, in the language of the tradition: Father, Son, and Holy Spirit.

It belongs to my prayer that this service of worship shall help us all toward a deepened appreciation of what our faith affirms when we worship the one true God as members of the community of the Holy Spirit of Jesus Christ, our Lord. Amen.

++++++++++++++++++++++++++++++++++

Announcements

I am Ruskin Falls, the minister here. With me in our sanctuary today are three other members of our church. David Harper, our church sexton, is working our video equipment. Sally Todd, our music director, is at the piano. And LaWanda Harris, who preached here last Sunday in my stead, is our liturgist today. And by the way, LaWanda, thank you for stepping in last week so that I could be away. I deeply appreciate your good work.

As the four of us gather here to prerecord this worship service to be shared with you next Sunday morning, it is a Friday afternoon. I don't know what turns our world might take between now and Sunday morning. Still, before moving on, I want to repeat some things I said in Thursday's congregational email and letter.

Right now in the United States, it's as if we took the time of the Spanish Flu pandemic of 1918, and the time of social, political, and cultural upheaval we call "the Sixties" (the 1960s), and put them together to get what's happening in this country today. At one and the same time, we are trying to come to terms both with the sudden, pandemic spread of the biological disease called COVID-19, against which, thus far, we have neither cure nor vaccine, and with the newly erupted turbulence that's been brought on by the social disease called racism, against which there *is* a cure and a vaccine, yet which disease we nevertheless strangely have tolerated, allowed to spread, and permitted to dominate, shape, and rule our nation from the start. And comparison of our situation with the Great Depression of the 1930s also can be made. Almost overnight, our unemployment rolls have skyrocketed. By the millions and millions, people's jobs, incomes, and livelihoods have either disappeared or undergone severe diminishment. Moreover, our houses of government seem less and less to be places deliberatively seeking the common good, and more and more to be mere battlegrounds for the will to power. All across the land, we are witnessing outbreaks of mob thinking and even violence. Our cities and neighborhoods are on the verge of becoming militarized. Trust in government to be of the people by the people for the people has grown thin. Trust in love to lead us forward is thinner still.

In the midst of all that, in today's sermon, I want to put in a good word for love. It's not that I naively believe that "love is all we need" to get us through the serious and horrible crises we are in. However, I do believe that God is love, and that the future that awaits us in the end is the future God's love intends. I also believe that that is not a future that we are passively to await, but, rather, a future whose cause we actively are to take up, a future that we actively are to serve, a future that we very actively are to work on behalf of in our time on Earth. In this sermon, I'll be talking about Christian kissing, divine triunity, and peace.

+ +

2ⁿᵈ Corinthians 13:11–13   *Holy kiss, triune God, and peace.*

Preface These are the closing lines of a letter addressed by the apostle Paul to the church in Corinth.

TEXT *(English translation: NRSV)*

Finally, brothers and sisters, farewell. Put things in order, listen to my appeal, agree with one another, live in peace; and the God of love and peace will be with you. Greet one another with a holy kiss. All the saints greet you.

The grace of the Lord Jesus Christ, the love of God, and the communion of the Holy Spirit be with all of you.

(1)

First, today, we'll address the matter of Christian kissing, then the question of divine triunity, then the appeal to live together in peace.

(2)

How many people have you ever greeted with a holy kiss? Do you even know what Paul has in mind when he tells us we ought to greet one another with a holy kiss? Here and in yet other places in the New Testament, it is written that we are to greet one another with a holy kiss—or as it's called in 1st Peter, a kiss of love. And, yet, while we're told in the Bible to greet one another with this exchange of kisses, it isn't something we nowadays do. Of course it would be understandable if we had temporarily desisted from such a practice, for example, due to the new coronavirus pandemic. There just are things that we Christians ought to be doing, that, under certain circumstances, we need to forego. Due to the present pandemic, it made good sense for in-person worship services to be put on hold for a while, and we plan to start back with in-person services when the time is right. However, we weren't exchanging kisses *before* the pandemic broke out. Biblical though it be, this is not a practice many, if any, of us in the church ever took up or intend to take up. Even those most insistent on strict obedience to the literal meaning of scripture don't insist that we should all be kissing each other in church. It simply doesn't bother Christians today—it doesn't even bother those who want to take scripture literally as God's words—that we no longer greet fellow Christians with the special kiss that we are told, in the New Testament, to greet one another with.

This reaction to Paul's words points to something important about how we read the Bible. It points to this fact: none of us take every sentence of scripture literally as a statement to be believed and obeyed at face value. Literally speaking, the Bible tells us we should greet our fellow Christians with a special kiss. But few, if any, of us today are prepared to do that—or even to stop and ask what a holy kiss might be. And we do not sense that we are violating the gospel of Jesus by not exchanging such kisses with one another. And that means we don't take Paul's words at face value as words we are obligated to believe and obey. And that means we don't really accept that every word of scripture is a word from God that we are to believe and obey at face value. For, if we did, then either we should be doing a whole lot more kissing with a whole lot more people, or else we should be feeling guilty for not doing that.

And the Bible is filled with verses that you and I don't take literally and at face value. How many of us consider every word of scripture to be a word from God that we are obligated to obey when we read in 1st Peter 3:3 that women shouldn't braid their hair and shouldn't wear either gold jewelry or fine clothes? Or when we read in 1st Corinthians 6:1 that Christians are not to get involved in lawsuits involving other Christians? Or when we hear Jesus say in Matthew 5:22 that if you call anyone a fool, you're going to hell? Or when he says in Luke 9:59, "Let the dead bury the dead"? Or when, in Luke 14:33, he says, "None of you can become my disciple if you do not give up all your possessions"?

For all of us, there are passages of scripture that we don't take literally at face value as a word from God that we are obligated to believe and obey. Nor should we! The Bible is not a collection of sentences that we are passively to accept as timeless truths or eternal commands. Rather, each passage of scripture is subject to interpretation, and different passages need to be interpreted in differing ways! Not all the verses of the Bible witness to the good news of Jesus Christ in the same manner, and not all verses guide us in the same fashion toward how Christians ought to live. Thus, we don't do scripture justice when we go to pulling verses from the Bible and insisting that they be accepted as all equally true and equally important teachings and commands. Rather, we always must ask how these words witness to the word of God that is the gospel of Jesus Christ. To talk about what a passage of scripture gives us to believe and do, we must engage in *interpretation* of the passage.

(3)

Now comes a somewhat different aspect of biblical interpretation: some things that are not explicitly stated in the Bible may nevertheless become valued guides to Christian faith and action. Some things that are nowhere spelled out in the Bible may nevertheless rightly be embraced as biblical truth. And one of those things is the doctrine of the Trinity.

Nowhere in the Bible does it state that God is triune. Nowhere in the Bible does the word "trinity" ever occur. Nowhere in the Bible does it say that God actually *is* what the traditional doctrine of the Trinity says God is, namely Father, Son, and Holy Spirit—or Creator, Redeemer, and Advocate (or Counselor)—all three at one and the same time. No passage in the Bible explicitly refers to God as "one God in three persons." And yet that is what the church came to affirm of God with its doctrine of the Trinity.

Yes, there are references to Jesus as the Son of God; and there are passages where he addresses God as Father, who rules over all things; and there is talk of God present with the church through the Holy Spirit. Moreover, there are a handful of passages, such as the one we're reading today, where Jesus, God, and the Holy Spirit are mentioned in the same breath. Still, neither this passage nor any of the others actually say what is claimed in the doctrine of the Trinity, namely that eternal God is one God in three eternally distinct ways of being God.

Here's the traditional doctrine in a nutshell: God is God the Father, who is not a part of but is wholly other than our world, who created all things out of nothing; and, at the same time, without ceasing to be the God who is wholly other than our world, God also is God the Son, who entered our world in the life of Jesus Christ, who was crucified by our world and who then was removed from the world not by death but through resurrection from death; and, at the same time, without ceasing to be the God who is wholly other than our world, and without ceasing to be the God who came into the world in Jesus, God also is God the Holy Spirit, who turns the witness and proclamation of the church into God's own word to us here and now, teaching, admonishing, comforting, healing, directing, and encouraging us that we might honor God's lordship and live as God's own children.

That's the doctrine of the Trinity in a nutshell. And, while no passage of scripture explicitly states that God is eternally one God in these three distinct ways of being God, the church has found itself brought to talk that way, because that's how God has revealed Godself to us.

Remember: what we know of God, we know because of God's act of self-revelation. God is not an object we one day might come upon or figure out in our minds; rather, God approaches us in all God's mystery as a subject who addresses us. Jesus did not come to us as a wise individual who plies us with interesting ideas about the possible existence and nature of God. Rather, he came as God's act of self-revelation. And Jesus did not found the church to be a good place for pondering the possible existence and nature of God. Rather, he founded the church to be how and where testimony to the gospel he came bringing is turned into the self-revelation of God's own word, mysteriously speaking itself into people's hearts and minds and lives today. Jesus was not on a quest, nor is the church on a quest, to find a possibly existent God. Rather, in Jesus and through the church's witness to him, the God who actually *is* reaches into the world and addresses us as Lord of all. Christian faith is not a search for a God who might or might not exist. Christian faith is a way of responding to the actuality of the God who, in Jesus and through the church's witness to the gospel of Jesus, speaks God's own word to us, revealing to us God's own reality, truth, and presence as Lord of all. Again, the doctrine of the Trinity is nowhere stated as such in the Bible. Rather, it is our way of saying what must be true of God for God to be this God who dwells in hiddenness before and beyond all things; who, at the same time, came among us in the life and mission of Jesus; who, at the same time, continues to reveal God's word and will and way through the witness of the church.

Of course, in an important sense, the doctrine of the Trinity is the church's confession of the mystery, even the incomprehensibility, of a God who is hidden beyond all worlds while at the same time revealed in the life and mission of Jesus and in the witness of the Holy Spirit. We don't know just what it means to say that God is eternally One in these Three and eternally these Three in One. However, that is the best we've come up with for confessing the divine activity that has announced itself in the life and mission of the child of Israel, Jesus Christ, and in the Spirit of the community, the church, that grew out of his life and mission.

And, too, there's this important aspect of God's triune being: If God is not simply one, but rather eternally these Three in One—if God is eternally this trinity of "persons," Father, Son, and Holy Spirit—that means that God never did, never does, and never shall exist in what you and I would call solitude or aloneness or isolation. Rather, God the Father, God the Son, and God the Holy Spirit are an eternal fellowship. God's oneness is eternally the oneness of divine communion among the three centers that are who God is. Even if God had never created the universe, or even if the universe should disappear, *God is never alone.* God is eternally a God engaged in fellowship, eternally a God engaged in communion, eternally a God in whom three divine centers share and celebrate life together. This is the meaning of the New Testament claim that *God is love*. It is not that, at some point, a lonely God decided to practice love and, so, created a world to love. Rather, from all eternity, God always *is* the love that unites God the Father, God the Son, and God the Holy Spirit. And whatever else that might mean, it means at least this: *Love really is of God*. In its deepest, truest, and most original sense, love is not of this world; rather, love is the very nature of God. This is to say that the deepest mystery and the greatest power in all the universe is the love that is taught by Jesus through the witness of his Holy Spirit—the love that now is yours and mine to know, enjoy, and share, here on Earth.

(4)

This brings me to Paul's appeal to *live in peace*.

The peace we are to live in goes hand in glove with the love God is and the future God's love intends—the future God's love is calling into being—the future Jesus called God's coming kingdom—the future that is in keeping with the love that God our Creator, God our Redeemer, God our Counselor, *is*. And the biblical word for that future is *peace*. We children of the triune God are to live here and now in keeping with the peace God's love intends.

The apostle Paul knows, however, and you and I need to realize, that the peace God's love intends runs deeper than merely superficial calm. The peace God's love intends is the peace that declares itself in these words from Psalm 85:10: "Steadfast love and faithfulness will meet; righteousness and peace will kiss each other." The peace God's love intends is peace that is kissed by righteousness. And, in the covenant traditions of Israel, that means *peace that is born of truthfulness before God and compassion toward others.* As the prophets of Israel declared and as Jesus proclaimed in their wake, peace kissed by righteousness is peace worked toward, peace striven for, peace reached a) through truthfulness before God regarding the blessings of this Earth that we have been privileged to enjoy, and b) through compassionate commitment to treating others as persons intended by God to enjoy Earth's blessings equally with us. In other words, this means a) being honest about the extent to which our relationship to Earth's blessings is godly and the extent to which it is sinful; and b) acknowledging that godliness entails compassionate commitment to the good God's love intends for all.

And this is difficult work! It requires letting go of I-me-mine long enough to join hands with those who are not thriving and flourishing as God's love intends. If I myself am not thriving and flourishing, it means keeping solidarity with others like me rather than seeking my fortune by climbing over them and leaving them behind. And for those of us who thrive and flourish in privileged ways, it especially includes joining hands with those cut off from the privileges we enjoy—by, for example, joining hands with the disabled and the disadvantaged, joining hands with the poor and needy, joining hands with the outcast and the downcast, joining hands with the sat-upon and spat-upon, joining hands with the injured and the maimed, joining hands with the down-and-out and hurting, joining hands with the persecuted and the oppressed. Peace kissed by righteousness is peace that comes of joining hands to form a togetherness of dignity and respect where all have realistic access to life's blessings and genuine opportunity to experience life on Earth as the gracious gift of God's wondrous love. Peace kissed by righteousness is the peace that reigns over the future that God's love is calling into being and calling us to serve. And that is the peace that the apostle Paul appeals to us to embrace.

Again, this peace runs deeper than merely superficial calm. For there are forces present in our world and even in ourselves that powerfully contend against the peace God's love intends— forces that even violently contest the coming of the time when all shall have realistic access to and genuine opportunity to enjoy the blessing that God intends for life on Earth to be for all. As happened with Jesus himself, so with us: taking up the cause of this peace demands readiness to contend with such forces and to contest both their arrogantly blatant and their deviously subtle ways of inflicting disadvantage and harm on God's children.

And I daresay that, as we in fact take up the cause of this peace—as we learn to serve this peace—we actually shall learn as well what it means to greet one another with a holy kiss, that biblical kiss of love in the name of the Father, and of the Son, and of the Holy Spirit. Amen.

15

Revelation 4:1–11   Why worship God?

June 14, 2020, 2nd Sunday after Pentecost

Greeting
The grace of the Lord Jesus Christ be with you all!

Sometimes we tend to forget it, and sometimes we seem strangely unwilling to admit it, but the truth of the matter is this: we humans need God's guidance, grace, and love if we are to know the world in all its fullness, enjoy life at its utmost best, and look death in the face with serene and faith-filled courage.

Worship is a way of being taught, a way of learning, to let ourselves be led by this wonderful though also mysterious God. It belongs to my prayer that this service of worship shall help us all to become more soundly and more intimately attuned both to the goodness and the mystery of God and to the humble boldness and bold humility that God desires for us to have and to live out and to inspire in others. Amen.

+ +

Announcements
I am Ruskin Falls. I serve here as minister, and ordinarily I do the preaching. I will, however, be away the next two Sundays, as I'll be serving as a commissioner to the Presbyterian Church (U.S.A.) General Assembly. I was supposed to be going to

Baltimore for that. However, because of COVID-19, all commissioners are staying home this year and working via Zoom. Still, I'll be away the next two Sundays. Filling the pulpit on June 21 will be a ministerial colleague of mine, Carol Clark, who is on the staff of the Presbytery of Arkansas. And filling the pulpit on June 28 will be one of our own members, LaWanda Harris, who herself is pursuing seminary studies in preparation for becoming a Presbyterian minister.

LaWanda also is with me in the sanctuary right now to serve as liturgist today. Also here are our music director and pianist, Sally Todd, and videographer, David Harper.

Speaking of liturgy: each week we send out a congregational email that provides the following things: a brief word from me regarding something or other, and, for the upcoming Sunday, the sermon text, the words to the unison confession of sin we will be praying, and the words to the unison affirmation of faith we will be saying. And Sally provides some helpful notes regarding the music that will be part of the service. You don't have to be a member here to be on our email list. If you are not on it yet, but would like to be, just send us an email letting us know that, and we'll be glad to include you in future emails.

And let me add this for those who've never been here in our sanctuary: while our session has not made a decision regarding the right time for our church to begin holding in-person worship services again, when we do start gathering here again, please know that we would love to meet you and let you get to meet us in person. For now, I'll share with you what we say about ourselves in our visitor brochure:

We are followers of Jesus Christ, striving together to serve the future ruled by the truth and grace of God.

In the power of the Holy Spirit, we seek not to be conformed to the world as it is, but to let our lives and world be transformed by the gospel Christ came bringing.

Here in Little Rock's Hillcrest Community, we seek to be a center of worship, theological learning, generosity, and courage, where hearts are lifted, minds stretched, and wills moved by the guidance and grace that God has spoken and speaks into the world through the life and mission of Jesus.

We see inclusiveness, the loving embrace of one another in and amidst our differences, as a visible sign of the new humanity that God is calling into being.

If you have questions about who we are or how we serve, feel free to ask them!

If you find yourself being drawn toward membership in our church, please let us know! In the meantime, know that you are invited and welcome to participate in the worship, teaching, and fellowship activities of our church any time, be it occasionally or be it on a more regular basis.

Come as you are, and grow in Christ.

+ +

Revelation 4:1–11　　　　　　　　　　*Why worship God?*

TEXT *(English translation: NRSV)*

After this I looked, and there in heaven a door stood open! And the first voice, which I had heard speaking to me like a trumpet, said, "Come up here, and I will show you what must take place after this." At once I was in the spirit, and there in heaven stood a throne, with one seated on the throne! And the one seated there looks like jasper and carnelian, and around the throne is a rainbow that looks like an emerald. Around the throne are twenty-four thrones, and seated on the thrones are twenty-four elders, dressed in white robes, with golden crowns on their heads. Coming from the throne are flashes of lightning, and rumblings and peals of thunder, and in front of the throne burn seven flaming torches, which are the seven spirits of God; and in front of the throne there is something like a sea of glass, like crystal.

Around the throne, and on each side of the throne, are four living creatures, full of eyes in front and behind: the first living creature like a lion, the second living creature like an ox, the third living creature with a face like a human face, and the fourth living creature like a flying eagle. And the four living creatures, each of them with six wings, are full of eyes all around and inside. Day and night without ceasing they sing, "Holy, holy, holy, the Lord God the Almighty, who was and is and is to come." And whenever the living creatures give glory and honor and thanks to the one who is seated on the throne, who lives forever and ever, the twenty-four elders fall before the one who is seated on the throne and worship the one who lives forever and ever; they cast their crowns before the throne, singing, "You are worthy, our Lord and God, to receive glory and honor and power, for you created all things, and by your will they existed and were created."

(1)

In the book of Revelation, an otherwise unknown Christian named John discloses visions that came to him while on the island of Patmos in the time of the Roman Empire. It appears that he had been forced into exile there because authorities believed his preaching was fomenting social unrest, instigating revolt against Roman law and order, and disrupting the imperial peace that Roman law and order was designed to secure. And throughout this book written by this political exile, the question looms large: Why worship God?

Admittedly it's not acts of worship that grab our attention on a first reading of Revelation. What first jumps out at us are the many unusual images it contains, such as in the passage we just read. Here God's heavenly throne is surrounded by twenty-four elders sitting on thrones and wearing crowns. Before God's throne are seven spirits and a sea of glass. And around that throne are four winged creatures full of eyes in back and in front—as well as within (whatever that might be like!). Throughout the book there occur scenes of plagues on Earth. There is one where much of Earth is burned away, one where the ocean turns to blood, one where sun and moon and stars lose much of their light, and one where an eagle flies around crying, "Woe to those who dwell on Earth!" And, there are yet other unusual figures who make an appearance. There are four figures on horseback, riding forth as harbingers of coming calamities; there's a dragon with seven heads, a monster from the sea, a monster from the earth, a beast that bears the number 666, numerous mysterious angels, and one hundred and forty-four thousand specially protected servants of God. There's also a bottomless pit, a lake of fire, a cosmic battlefield called Armageddon, and a new Jerusalem that, in the end, comes descending to Earth from heaven. The book is filled with unusual, even strange and bizarre, images. Clearly these images are intended as symbols. They don't mean what they are; they mean what they are about. And to understand Revelation, we need to understand what they're about.

I am aware that many preachers treat John's symbols as coded predictions that, when properly decoded, turn out to be about people and events in our own time. That, however, is a misguided reading of this book. John was not out to baffle his fellow Christians with symbols that, for two thousand years, no one would understand. His first readers knew what these symbols concerned, namely the call of Jesus Christ in a world that is antagonistic to Jesus Christ. More specifically, they knew these symbols identified Roman rulers, Roman politics, Roman culture, and the Roman economy as beastly adversaries of Jesus and his followers. They knew that these symbols concerned the struggle that they as Christians must take up in order to keep the church from becoming pushed aside, swallowed up, or otherwise reduced to irrelevance by the politics, marketplace, and culture of the Roman Empire. They knew that John was staking this claim: We can't be equally allegiant to the future that Jesus called God's coming kingdom, and to the present ways of the Roman Empire; we can't be loyal to Jesus and the emperor at the same time.

In the New Testament, there are also other voices on this issue. There are voices that don't treat following Jesus and being a compliant citizen as so exclusive of each other. The warning in Revelation, however, is this: between our Christian calling and our culture's social, political, and economic allure, there is tremendous tension and colossal antagonism. And behind all the strange imagery we meet with here, behind John's many unusual symbols, and behind his political position-taking, is this question: Why worship God?

(2)

In chapter four, John tells of being lifted into the throne room of heaven. That doesn't mean he was transported physically to heaven. Rather he was transported, as he puts it, "in the spirit," which is to say in a visionary experience. What then is given to John to see is this: in heaven, God is unceasingly worshiped, and the song is constantly and passionately sung: "Holy, holy, holy, the Lord God the Almighty, who was and is and is to come...creator of all things. You are worthy, our Lord and God, to receive glory and honor and power, for you created all things, and by your will they existed and were created."

From that point on, Revelation, including all the odd images and symbols that then show up, is an unfolding of what it means, here on Earth, to do what is done in heaven, namely to dwell in worshipful centeredness on God.

Let's talk about worship. We can talk another time about the beasts and battles and blood and other symbolism that come flying at us in Revelation. What we need to do today is take notice of what John recognizes in his opening vision of heaven. What John sees is this: worshiping God is the main activity that goes on in heaven. In heaven, worship isn't just an occasional thing; it's what goes on constantly and always; moreover, it's what life on Earth should be about. Life on Earth should be about *striving to become truly worshipfully centered on God.*

(3)

Why does God desire to be worshiped? Why does God desire our adoration and praise? Why do we so often, in the Bible, bump up against God commanding people to worship God and to worship no one and nothing else? Why does God desire our adoration, our praise, our worship?

Let's start with this: it is not that God needs our adoration and praise for God's sake, in order to make God feel powerful, mighty, important, respected, meaningful, triumphant, or glad to be God. God isn't driven by envy or by low self-esteem or by insecurity or by selfish pride to need our service of worship. God isn't even driven by a need for company—God doesn't need for us to worship God to keep God from being lonely. God is triune! As the God who is at one and the same time the three ways of being God the tradition has called Father, Son, and Holy Spirit, God never was and never will be lonely. In short, God doesn't need our adoration and praise to make God feel right or good or delighted about being God. God could be God very well, thank you, without praise and adoration from us. God does not need our service of worship for God's sake, as if God otherwise can't be content being God.

And yet, there *is* this sense in which God *does* need our worship: God needs our worship because God has created the world out of divine love. Let me explain.

God would have been perfectly fine delighting for all eternity in the triune fellowship of love that is shared in God as Father, Son, and Holy Spirit. However, God let God's love spill over into creating something that could have life apart from God, something that isn't God, something radically different from God, something free to have its own way of being, free to have its own life, independently of God. That something is our world. That something is the human life that you and I are part of. The Earth and those who dwell therein have been created to be loved by God. God didn't have to create us, but God did. And God did so as a pure gift—the gift of letting beings other than God have the opportunity to experience being alive and knowing and enjoying and sharing in God's goodness. God created us that God might share with us the love God is. God did not create us to be puppets manipulated by God or machines programed to do God's bidding. Rather, God created us to be creatures free to explore life on our own, free to discover the world on our own, free to mature into our own being, free to wonder, free to ask questions, free to experiment, free to come to our own conclusions, free to take responsibility for our life together on Earth, and free—not forced, but free—to worship God.

And why worship God? For starters, because, as the voices sing in John's vision of heaven, the God whose will and way are revealed in Jesus Christ is worthy of worship. Like nothing and no one in this world, the God revealed in Jesus Christ is worthy of worship.

Think about it: God created us to love us purely. Human existence is God's gift of the opportunity to know, enjoy, and share God's love. And God's love is pure in a way no human love is. God loves you with a love that has only your and your world's truly best interests at heart. God loves you with a love that is set only on bringing out in you what God knows is truly best about you—and God knows you better than you yourself or anyone else on Earth can know you! Human love, as wonderful as it is, is not pure love. Human love is complexly conditional love. It's always affected and conditioned by something about the beloved, and by what we do or don't receive in return from the beloved, and by what the beloved does with our love. Human love is always entangled in complex webs of self-interest, self-importance, ignorance, self-deception, and lies that prevent us from ever having purely the truly best interests of others at heart. Human love, even at its self-giving best, is always also shaped by conditions that prevent us from having purely the truly best interests of others at heart.

God's love for us is otherwise. God has no ulterior motives, no hidden agenda, no interests of God's own that we must serve before God loves us. God's love for us is unconditional—and this despite the fact that God knows all there is to know about us, including how indifferent and even opposed to God's love we actually tend to be, and how entangled in self-interest, self-importance, ignorance, self-deception, and lies our relationships here on Earth tend to become. God knows us better than anyone on Earth, better even than we know ourselves. God knows the truth about us. And God's desire is purely this: to bring out in us what truly is best about us, and to bring out in our world what truly is best about our world.

Which brings me back to this: *God is worthy of worship!* God is worthy of worship because: God, and God alone, knows the truth about us. God, and God alone, loves us unconditionally. God, and God alone, has our and our world's truly best interests at heart. God, and God alone, desires purely to bring out in us what truly is best about us, and to bring out in our world what truly is best about our world. And the way we learn what God knows about us, and the way we become opened to God's unconditional love, and the way we discover what truly is best about us and about our world, and the way we are enabled to grow into God's love and draw our world into God's love as well is through true worship of God.

Worship is about singing and praying and speaking and listening and doing also other things and being joined together in ways that help us to stop thinking from a center in ourselves, and to begin thinking from a center that is in God's pure love for the world. Worship is engagement in the activities and practices that have nurtured in and among us eyes and ears for the reality, truth, and presence of *God*, speaking God's word into our lives, teaching us what God sees in us and what God knows is truly best about us, and changing—even transforming—us by creating in us growing openness for God's unconditional love, and greater awareness of the things in our world that are in need of change and transformation through God's love.

We can look more closely some other time at John's visions of beasts and battles and blood and other disconcerting sightings. I think it important, however, before doing that, to get clear about this: behind John's writing is this threefold conviction: we were given life that we might learn, enjoy, and share the love of God revealed in Jesus Christ; that is unconditional love that has our and our world's truly best interests at heart; and the way we humans move toward and grow in that love is by centering life worshipfully on God—through singing and praying and speaking and listening and being together in ways that let the truth of God's love break through the complex webs of self-interest, self-importance, ignorance, self-deception, and lies that we have become entangled in and that we've entangled our world in.

Basic to Revelation is this twofold theme: First, when we *don't* work at letting our lives become centered and constantly recentered on God through divine worship, we inevitably end up centering our lives and our world on things that, in the end, diminish and harm the human spirit with tragic and even beastly consequences. Secondly, as we do learn centeredness on God through true worship, our reward will be this: a courage and serenity stronger than anything anyone or anything in this world could ever give us—the courage and serenity of knowing—deep down in our souls, really knowing—how safely sheltered we finally really are, in the grace, love, and future of Jesus Christ, who has revealed to us eternal God's wonderfully good and graciously loving will for the world.

For all the catastrophes, calamities, beasts, and other strange figures and events in Revelation, the point of this (in many ways strange and bizarre) piece of writing is to give us promise, hope, and even joy. John wants us to realize that true knowledge of God awakens in us an astonishing sense of courage and serenity, even in the face of the most painful setbacks, the most agonizing sorrows, the most bitter sufferings, and the most hideous forms of evil this world could ever send our way. And true knowledge of God comes from life that has its center in true worship of God. Which is why we must be ever on our guard not to let the church's service of worship become pushed aside, swallowed up, or otherwise reduced to irrelevance, by the politics, marketplace, and culture of any worldly power.

True worship, John would have us understand, is about gathering before invisible God in honest reverence, awe, and humility, to let ourselves be made more open to God's mysterious, sacred, and holy presence among us, speaking God's own word into our hearts and minds and lives through the crucified yet resurrected Jesus, and declaring, "I love you. Unconditionally. Follow me. And be generous with your life. And be at peace. And have courage. For truly I am with you always." Always! Amen.

16

Jeremiah 6:10, 13–15a   The way forward.

July 5, 2020, 5ᵗʰ Sunday after Pentecost

Greeting
The grace of the Lord Jesus Christ be with you all!

We here at Pulaski Heights Presbyterian Church are a once-upon-a-time very large congregation that presently is a rather small congregation. We are a congregation that once drew lots of water from the wells of youthful vigor and energy, and, right now, we're a congregation drawing most of its water from the wells of the wisdom and experience of members who, however youthful in spirit, are well beyond the days of their youth—and past the midpoint of their time on this Earth. We are a member congregation of a denomination, the Presbyterian Church (U.S.A.), that once was known as, but that no longer is, a mainstream mover and shaker of American religious life. We are a congregation whose mission may feel less clear to us right now than it did among those who were here just a few decades ago, when we numbered over eight hundred members. Still, the church back in New Testament times was very small and very poor, and its members simply trusted in Jesus's word to them: "Y'all are the light of the world."

Now Jesus is depending on you and me and lots of other congregations like us, to be that light.

And so, as we say in our visitor brochure,

Here in Little Rock's Hillcrest community,
we seek to be a center of
worship, theological learning, generosity, and courage,
where hearts are lifted, minds stretched, and wills moved
by the guidance and grace
that God has spoken and speaks into the world
through the life and mission of Jesus.

It belongs to my prayer that God will continue to bless us with the faith and the audacity to go on doing precisely that, filled with the joyful confidence that we have learned through the history of Jesus Christ, which history includes the history of the law and the prophets of Israel that, as Jesus said in his Sermon on the Mount, he came not to destroy but to fulfill. Amen.

+ +

Announcements

I am Ruskin Falls. It is my privilege to serve as minister for this amazing congregation. Joining me in our sanctuary today are our music director and pianist, Sally Todd; choir member Mary Kai Clark, who will be leading us in singing; videographer David Harper; and, as our liturgist, LaWanda Harris.

Let me take just a moment to say something that I was supposed to mention in this past week's congregational email, but that I failed to include in it: our church treasurer, Randy Gates, has prepared midyear giving statements to send out this week, so that we all can compare our own year-to-date giving records with his. If there's a discrepancy between your records and his, or if you have any questions at all regarding gifts to the

church or our church finances in general, please feel free to give
Randy a call at the church office. He'll be glad to go over any
and all of that with you.

Note, too, you don't have to be a member of this church
to receive our weekly congregational email. If you'd like to be
added to our list, just send us an email saying that, and we'll
gladly begin sending you our emails.

+ +

Jeremiah 6:10, 13–15a   *The way forward.*

TEXT *(English translation: NRSV)*
> To whom shall I speak and give warning, that they
> may hear? See, their ears are closed, they cannot listen.
> The word of the Lord is to them an object of scorn; they
> take no pleasure in it...
>
> For from the least to the greatest of them, everyone
> is greedy for unjust gain; and from prophet to priest,
> everyone deals falsely. They have treated the wound of
> my people carelessly, saying, "Peace, peace," when there
> is no peace. They acted shamefully, they committed
> abomination; yet they were not ashamed, they did not
> know how to blush.

(1)

These are not atheists or pagans that Jeremiah is addressing
here. These are members of his own faith community. It is
believers in the Lord God of Israel to whom Jeremiah declares,

"Your ears are closed to God's word! You have ceased to listen for God's word! You have failed to hear and heed God's word!"

There are, here, three charges that Jeremiah levels against the community of faith.

(2)

One charge is this: *the word of the Lord is to them an object of scorn.*

It's not that they deride or ridicule God's word. They simply believe they already know enough about what God has to say to be able to figure things out on their own from this point. As a result, they aren't genuinely open to hearing anything *new*, *different*, or *unexpected* from God. They don't spurn God's word by denying it. Rather, they spurn God's word by being *blasé* about it—by not listening in the expectation of hearing something new and life-changing regarding God, or something new and mind-altering regarding themselves, or something new and world-transforming regarding humankind. Think about it: if, while you are talking to me, I act as if you have nothing to say that I don't already know—if I act as if there's nothing more that I actually need to hear from you—if I act as if you can't really have anything new to teach me—then, in an important sense, I have scorned what you are saying. I have belittled what you are saying by treating it as something I can just as well ignore. Likewise, declared Jeremiah, God's word has become for the faith community an object of scorn. For, no matter how much they honor God's word with their lips, they are not open to hearing from God something that might change, alter, or transform how they think, how they feel, how they act, and how they live together.

And what about you and me? Are we genuinely open to learning something new from God regarding God's will and way and regarding ourselves and our life together? Or do we casually presume that we already know all we need to know about God's word? Do we worship, pray, and study with a readiness to be surprised by God? Or do we presume a familiarity with God's word that closes us off to anything surprising, re-directional, and transformative? Are we truly open to being taught by God's word something new, something surprising, something that calls forth rebirth and redirection in our lives and world? Or have we closed ourselves off to the very possibility of such an experience?

(3)

A second charge against the community of faith is this: *they take no pleasure in God's word.*

That doesn't mean they experience God's word as unpleasant. Rather, they don't let it evoke in them the attitude of wonder, awe, reverence, courage, and obedience that the scriptures call, at one and the same time, the *fear of the Lord* and *delight in God's will and way.* They react not passionately but passionlessly when God declares, "You profoundly need to know, and yet, apart from my word you cannot know, why you're here or what your life ultimately means or what happens when you die! This passing world can't tell you these things! So, do not be conformed to the world, but be transformed by the renewing of your minds as you let yourself be taught, challenged, judged, changed, and directed by this assurance from me, the Lord your God: You were created to know, enjoy, and share my eternal love. My love was your beginning, and my love awaits you at this life's end. Delight, now, in knowing that, and go where my love leads, and do what my love would have you do!" That assurance and admonition belongs to God's word. However, declares Jeremiah, the community of faith now takes greater delight in conforming to the expectations, attitudes, and ways of the world around it than in conforming the world to the expectations, attitudes, and ways that are called for by God's word. The community of faith is letting itself be more defined by the world than by God's word.

And what about us? Does God's word evoke in us the attitude of wonder, awe, reverence, courage, and obedience that the scriptures call the *fear of the Lord* and *delight in God's will and way*? Or are we so set on accommodating ourselves to the expectations, attitudes, and ways of the world around us that we delight more in conforming to the world than in conforming the world to God's word? Does God's word fire us with enthusiasm for our identity as both beneficiaries and agents of God's love? Or do we look first and foremost to the world around us to tell us who we are and what our life should be about?

(4)

A third charge against the community of faith is this: *they committed abomination, yet they were not ashamed; they did not know how to blush.*

That doesn't mean the people of God were brazenly doing what they knew they shouldn't do. It doesn't mean they intentionally opposed God's will and way. It was more a matter of feeling no embarrassment or shame, simply because they saw no wrong and no harm in what they were doing.

They presumed themselves nice enough, good enough, decent enough, godly enough, to feel sure that God was on their side and supportive of their customs, institutions, and national undertakings. And in this regard, they did prove terribly, terribly wrong. For, toward the end of Jeremiah's life, the homeland of the children of Israel was overrun by the armies of the king of Babylon; the countryside was ransacked; the Holy City of Jerusalem was destroyed; Israelites were driven into exile; and the nation of Israel ceased to exist. Jeremiah had prophesied the coming of such a disaster. It was coming, he had declared, as the consequence of the ungodliness that had come to pervade Israelite society. Israel, you see, had first been gathered by God in the land of Canaan as a covenant community of neighborly and equally free persons. No privileged elite were to be allowed to rule or dominate the populace. However, by the time of Jeremiah, a ruling class had indeed come to dominate. The king who sat on the throne, and his relatives; the priests who ran the temple, and their relatives; the prophets whom the king trusted to be his counselors (which did *not* include Jeremiah!); and the families that now managed Israelite commerce—these together now formed a ruling elite that spelled the end of the old covenant community of neighborly and equally free persons. Over time, the privileged few at the top grew ever wealthier and more powerful, while the 90 percent of the population at the bottom slid ever further into poverty and suffering. Moreover, the dishonesty, greed, and unfairness at the top came to infect the whole social fabric. Israel's ancient sense of covenant community became so eroded through those at the top that even those *not* at the top lost their neighborly trust in one another. And God, declared Jeremiah, was going to let Israel reap the tragic consequences of the kind of society and nation they had become.

That day came when Israel's rulers finally did find themselves seriously at cross-purposes with the far wealthier and far more powerful king of Babylon, who then sent his armies in for the kill. It was following the destruction of Israel by Babylon that some members of the Israelite community of faith did come to see that being God's people is not about God being "on our side," but, rather, about letting God's word make a radical difference in our lives—a radical difference that, in turn, makes a radical difference in our world. They came to see that being God's people is about letting God's word turn us into persons who take God's ways more to heart than we take the ways of the world. It's about letting God's word turn us into servants of the future God's word intends, when every heart in every part of all creation shall be filled to overflowing with God's love. God, they came to see, isn't willy-nilly "on our side." Rather, God is out to draw us to God's side.

And what about you and me? Do we presume that we're so nice, so good, so decent, and so godly that we can rest assured that God is on our side and surely applauding the customs, institutions, and undertakings that presently define us as a people? Do we hear in God's word only confirmation of the goodness and godliness we want to see in ourselves and our society and our land? Or does God's word come at us as a word that calls in question and challenges how we think and feel and act and live as individuals, as a society, and as a nation? Do we hear in God's word merely God's yes to what we already believe or want to believe about God and about ourselves and about our world? Or do we hear God's word coming at us as a word that's out to transform our understanding, our attitudes, our ways, and our world?

(5)

Having noted how his people have failed to hear and heed God's word aright, Jeremiah describes the result of that failure with these words: *they have treated the wound of my people carelessly, saying, "Peace, peace," when there is no peace.*

Not being truly open to being taught by God's word, being set on protecting the privileges they enjoy in the world as it is, expecting from God's word only a yes to what they already believe about God and about themselves and about the ways of the world—all this, declares Jeremiah, has resulted in the festering of what he calls *the wound of my people.* And "the wound of my people" is Jeremiah's term for what today is called social injustice.

When Jeremiah talks about "the wound of my people," he's talking about the social inequality, the elitist rule, and the forms of economic exploitation that had become business-as-usual in Israel. As we just observed, in the Israel of Jeremiah's time, a privileged portion of the population were enjoying power, wealth, security, and prosperity at the expense of those who didn't lead so privileged a life. Sometimes openly and sometimes deceptively and sometimes probably self-deceptively, those living comfortably at the top of the social ladder managed to manipulate law and order, managed to finagle finances and taxation, and managed to sway the institutions and ways of the religious establishment into serving their self-interests while they closed their eyes to and turned their backs on the living conditions of the non-privileged folks below them. One portion of the population was exercising social, political, and economic power in ways that protected their privileged position in society at the expense of and to the detriment of the livelihood and well-being of those below them on the social ladder. A relatively small number of "haves" were using the political machinery, religious institutions, and economic system of Israel to make themselves more prosperous and secure, even though what they were doing left the "have-nots" leading lives haunted by adversity, inequity, insecurity, and desperation, at the bottom of a social ladder where there were no rungs for climbing to the top.

In other words, what Jeremiah calls "the wound of my people" is this: the hardship and indignity that so many of his people were suffering because those who did enjoy prosperity and power were turning their backs on the rights and needs of those socially and economically beneath them. Israel now was pervaded by attitudes and ways that surely mocked the ways of equality and love of neighbor that God always intended Israel to serve.

As justification for not trying to usher in major changes, many from among Israel's privileged class were saying this to Jeremiah: "Look, Jeremiah, God mainly wants God's people to live in peace. And we who now are in power are good at preserving the peace. We've diplomatically protected Israel against the schemes of foreign rulers, without hindering Israel's international trade. And within our borders we've seen to it that our people needn't fear any outbreaks of civil unrest or revolution. We're not a nation at war; we're not a society riddled with violence. We're at peace. Let's keep it that way!"

To which Jeremiah, throughout his lifetime, declared, "But this isn't genuine peace! Genuine peace is not simply the absence of conflict, violence, and war. Genuine peace is about commitment to treating all people equally, fairly, and justly as God's beloved children. Genuine peace is about taking active steps to dismantle any social structures, institutions, and attitudes that allow one part of the population to lord it over others by cultivating privileges for themselves that the others don't have. Peace without commitment to taking such steps as these is and always will be superficial, is and always will be 'peace, peace, when there is no peace,' is and always will be a peace that cannot last. It will not be the peace that God intends. It will not be the peace God's word commands."

(6)

Without going into it any further today, let me close simply by noting that Jeremiah's point here is twofold.

On the one hand, a society that is marked by "the wound of my people," a society that is marked by social injustice, a society that is divided into those with privileged access to power, wealth, and security, and those without such access, is a society that still has a lot to learn about hearing and heeding God's word. On the other hand, where people do strive to heal the wound of their people—where people do strive against social injustice—where people do strive to dismantle social attitudes, institutions, and arrangements that result in lives haunted by adversity, inequity, insecurity, and desperation at the bottom of a social ladder where there are no rungs for climbing to the top—if their striving is not grounded in hearing and heeding God's word, they are not on the road to lasting peace. For the road to lasting peace is the road to the future where every heart in every part of all creation is filled to overflowing with God's love. And the only way of getting there is by being guided there by God's own word—God's own life-changing, mind-altering, and world-transforming word.

Blessed are those who dare to learn to listen for and do what God is giving them to hear. For they are the way forward. Amen.

(17)

Matthew 19:1–6   Whom God has joined.

July 12, 2020, 6th Sunday after Pentecost

Greeting
The grace of the Lord Jesus Christ be with you all!

Worship services typically *close* with a benediction. I'd like to *begin* today with a benediction.

It's a benediction that comes from the Franciscan tradition—the tradition of St. Francis of Assisi. It goes like this:

> May God bless you with discomfort at
> easy answers, half-truths, and superficial relationships,
> so that you may live deep within your heart.

> May God bless you with anger at
> injustice, oppression, and exploitation of people,
> so that you may work for justice, freedom, and peace.

> May God bless you with tears to shed for those who suffer
> from pain, rejection, starvation, and war,
> so that you may reach out your hand
> to comfort them and turn their pain into joy.

And may God bless you with enough foolishness
to believe that you can make a difference in this world,
so that you can do what others claim cannot be done.

Amen.

+ +

Announcements

I'm Ruskin Falls, the minister here at Pulaski Heights
Presbyterian Church. Joining me in our sanctuary today are three
other members of our congregation. Serving as liturgist today is
Charles Gray; playing piano is our music director, Sally Todd;
and working our audio and video equipment is David Harper.

When, at the end of last March, we knew the outbreak
of COVID-19 meant we needed to stop gathering in person
for worship, it was clear that we should immediately begin
providing video worship services on our website. We just
weren't sure how. We're not a particularly technologically savvy
congregation—and I myself am too much of a Luddite to be a
techie type whatsoever at all. But we've worked hard at making
so-called "virtual worship" a possibility for our congregation.
We're not very fancy in what we do. But when the few of us
gather here every Friday afternoon to video a service for the
following Sunday, we try to be as true as we can to what we'd
be doing, were we all here together face-to-face. And what we
do in the making of each video, we do with all our members
here with us in our hearts, along with our heartfelt longing for
the day when worship finally can be in person again.

I don't know when that's going to be. Right now, the COVID-19 numbers here in Arkansas aren't such that a whole lot of our members—given the age and health conditions of so many of us—can feel comfortable with the thought of attending in person again very soon. And, yet, at the same time, everyone's desire to be back together runs broad and deep. So, we'll see. In the meantime, we'll carry on as best we can with what we're doing, working to improve on what we're doing, as we can, when we can. And, yes, even when we do return to in-person worship, the thought right now is, even then, to continue providing online worship for those who are unable to attend—or who are unready at that point to return to attending—in person.

Anyone who has worshiped here before knows that we're a congregation for whom this thing called "social distancing" just doesn't feel like who we are. And probably, for those of us who are here on Friday afternoons making these videos, the moment that seems most unlike our usual services is when we pass the peace of Christ. We ordinarily would be doing that with a lot of getting up and moving around and face-to-face hugs and handshakes—and maybe even some holy kisses! Being "socially distanced" just isn't us. Nevertheless, the congregational faith, hope, love, and courage that we've been blessed to know, is, I'm convinced, going to get us where we as a church need to be going, doing the things we need to do—including being "a center of worship, theological learning, generosity, and courage, where hearts are lifted, minds stretched, and wills moved by the guidance and grace that God has spoken and speaks into the world though the life and mission of Jesus."

+ +

Matthew 19:1–6   *Whom God has joined.*

TEXT *(English translation: NRSV)*

When Jesus had finished saying these things, he
left Galilee and went to the region of Judea beyond the
Jordan. Large crowds followed him, and he cured them
there.

Some Pharisees came to him, and to test him they
asked, "Is it lawful for a man to divorce his wife for any
cause?" He answered, "Have you not read that the one
who made them at the beginning 'made them male and
female,' and said, 'For this reason a man shall leave his
father and mother and be joined to his wife, and the
two shall become one flesh'? So they are no longer two,
but one flesh. Therefore what God has joined together,
let no one separate."

(1)

What I'm asking you to focus on with me today is not so much
the matter of marriage, as the question of how we listen for
God's *word*, God's *will*, God's *command*. I do plan to say a few
things about marriage as a social institution. After that, though,
I want mainly for us to give thought to how we hear and heed
God's call. First, though, let's turn to the matter of marriage.

We'll start with this: marriage is a legal contract that falls
under the civil jurisdiction of the state.

The state has a vested interest in regulating, with legal force
and recourse, certain of the privileges and responsibilities of
its citizens. For the sake of preserving a well-ordered society,
the state has a vested interest in having, among other things,

laws regarding what constitutes sexual decency and indecency, laws regarding parental claims and the responsibilities of parents to their children, laws regarding the establishment and enforcement of financial obligations, laws regarding who shall make medical decisions for those not in position to do so for themselves, and laws regarding how property may be allocated and passed on to others. And, the state has a vested interest in marriage as a civil contract in which people take on certain obligations to each other in exchange for certain privileges together, and in which they are granted certain privileges together in exchange for taking on certain obligations to each other. The state has a vested interest in marriage as a social institution that is established, recognized, and—not in all, but in certain respects—regulated by the laws of the state.

To be legally married—for a relationship to be established, recognized, and regulated *as* marriage under the law—a marriage contract (or license) must be officially recorded with the state. In this country, the state authorizes various persons to act as agents of its civil jurisdiction in recording marriage contracts. Judges and justices of the peace, for example, are legally authorized to play this role. Persons ordained to the ministry of particular religious communities also typically are authorized to play this role. I, for example, as an ordained minister for the Presbyterian Church (U.S.A.), have credentials from the state of Arkansas authorizing me to conduct a service of matrimony within this state and to record people's relationship as that of legally married. That is to say, for the sake of joining persons contractually in legal matrimony, I am authorized to act as an agent of the state. The state cannot require me to record marriage contracts, but it can and has authorized me to do so, if and when I choose to do that.

Our denomination, the Presbyterian Church (U.S.A.), also permits me to do this, though it does place certain requirements on me. For example, those asking me to conduct a wedding service for them must meet the requirements of the civil jurisdiction in which they intend to marry; they must engage in a series of meetings with me to discuss the nature of marriage and the church's teachings regarding the values a marriage should accord with; then, if I am satisfied that there is sufficient understanding, responsibility, and commitment behind their decision to marry, the church permits me, during a service of matrimony, to play the role of state agent and, on behalf of the state, record the marriage contract, thus permitting them to live legally married.

Typically, among us Presbyterians, a wedding service includes such things as a statement on the meaning of marriage, individual declarations of intent to marry, a scripture reading and meditation, an exchange of vows, and the minister's announcement of marriage. Then, recalling the words of Jesus that we heard in today's scripture reading, the minister typically declares, "Those whom God has joined together, let no one separate."

(2)

Question: Does my act of conducting someone's wedding— does my act of recording their marriage contract—or, for that matter, does their act of saying, "I do," necessarily mean that *God* has joined them together?

Interestingly, it is not unusual for Christians to equate the two. It is commonplace for Christians to equate being legally married with having been joined together by God. Yet, the two are not the same! Just because *I* have ritually joined certain people in marriage, and just because the state recognizes them as joined in marriage, doesn't mean that God has joined them.

Even if someone's decision to marry is marked by marvelous depths of understanding, responsibility, and commitment, neither my act of joining them together ritually, nor their saying "I do," nor my recording of their marriage contract with the state necessarily means that God has joined them. Nowhere do we have it on divine authority that my ritual joining of persons together necessarily means they have been joined by God. Nowhere do we have it on divine authority that saying "I do" necessarily means that they have been joined by God. Nowhere do we have it on divine authority that the state's recognition that someone is legally married necessarily means it was God's will for those particular persons to marry. Just because a minister has joined them, or just because they feel a deep commitment to each other, or just because the state declares them joined, doesn't necessarily mean that God has called them to turn their individual lives into the life of marriage.

Sabine and I were ritually joined in marriage by a Presbyterian minister, who then recorded our marriage with the state. We became legally married. Does that mean that God, at that time, joined us together? Does it mean that marrying each other was God's will for our lives? Does it mean that God had been speaking into our hearts and minds, saying, "Get married!"? Not necessarily! Whatever brought us to that point, however good we felt about getting married, however convinced we were that we were doing the right thing, that doesn't necessarily mean that turning our separate lives into a life together in marriage was God's will for us. It doesn't necessarily mean that our getting married involved hearing and heeding aright the guidance and direction that God was speaking into our hearts and minds. Even if getting married felt good and right to us, nevertheless, just because something feels good or right doesn't mean it is God's will that we do it. There are lots of things that lots of people feel good and right about doing that nevertheless surely are not God's will!

So: how can any of us know that we have been joined together in marriage by God?

It does make sense to me to think that, if we feel we have a good marriage, then surely that must mean that we've been joined by God. If, for example, we love each other, desire each other's presence and intimacy, are passionate about each other's good, share important values and ideals, strive more to understand and appreciate each other than to argue with and criticize each other, etc., then surely that must mean that we've been joined together by God. Surely a marriage that makes people feel good in these ways sounds like something willed by God. Surely that sounds like people whom God has joined together. Surely the presence of that kind of love, desire, passion, commonality, and respect strongly suggests a marriage that was God's will. Surely, at any rate, such things as these would be in keeping with God's intentions for marriage generally, and maybe even so in keeping with God's intentions as to give us every right to feel certain that these are people who've been joined together by God. In fact, even if it was without the ritual blessings of a minister and without the legal blessings of the state, that sure sounds like people who have been joined together by God.

That said, though, we need to remember this: what God desires for us isn't always what we want for ourselves. Sometimes, God calls us to take a path, to chart a course, to engage in a pursuit, to take an action, that's going to cost us some degree of pain, hardship, sacrifice, and suffering. God's rule is not, "If it feels good, it was my will." God's rule is, "If what you do is my will, you can feel good about doing it, even if it causes you pain, hardship, sacrifice, and suffering." A marriage that makes us feel good about ourselves still can put us on a path that wasn't God's will. On the other hand, a marriage that is personally difficult or perhaps a marriage that incurs considerable social scorn may nevertheless be the relationship that God intended for us, the relationship that God willed, the relationship that God was calling us to enter. For that matter, a marriage that we feel we didn't so much choose as get forced into may actually be a marriage that God was calling us to enter and, in this sense, a marriage of persons God has joined together.

Again, the question: how can we know whether or not we have been joined by God? How can we be sure that God is calling us to this particular marriage and not to another? Or how can we be sure whether God is calling us to marry at all, or whether God perhaps actually is calling us to remain unmarried?

And, again, the short answer is this: of ourselves, we do not and cannot know for sure. It is not built into the human heart, mind, soul, or spirit to know for sure, to know for certain, to know beyond question God's will for our life, God's call, God's word to us regarding what God desires to see us do.

(3)

I realize that that may sound like a shockingly negative conclusion. It may leave us thinking: why concern ourselves with God's will at all? If we can't be sure about God's will, why bother seeking it? If we can't be sure what God is calling us to do, why try to hear and heed God's call?

I find a helpful response to such questioning in something that actually was written for our own church's visitor brochure. Let me expand on that at this time.

Even though we ourselves can't say just how the experience happens, our core experience in the church, our core experience as part of the community of Jesus Christ's resurrection Spirit, is our experience of the gospel of Jesus breaking into our life in a way that nothing merely in and of this world ever could. It is given to us in the church to experience the gospel of Jesus coming at us as eternal God's own gracious and loving word. It is given to us in the church to experience eternal God addressing us through the gospel of Jesus to comfort, challenge, and direct us in redeeming ways—for example, by taking the ambiguity, anxiety, resentment, and fear that have come to rule so much of human life and turning it into a faith, hope, love, and courage that liberates us from destructive and self-destructive ways, and that breathes mysteriously wondrous enthusiasm, exuberance, and zest into our time on Earth. No, this doesn't rid us of questions, uncertainties, and doubts regarding the purpose, meaning, and course of our life.

However, as we let our questions, uncertainties, and doubts be brought into contact with the gospel of Jesus Christ—as the ambiguity, anxiety, resentment, and fear that mark so much of human life are brought into contact with God's word to the world in Jesus Christ—Christ's own Holy Spirit goes to work transforming all that into a faith, hope, love, and courage that frees us for a radically different life. And in that experience, we know that, even if we don't have absolutely certain answers to all our questions regarding God's word and will and way, we nevertheless now take up those questions, we now wrestle with those questions, under eternal God's own gracious, loving, and redeeming influence. We now know that it isn't simply worldly forces that are at work among us but also the otherworldly God of the gospel of Jesus.

Even if our own sense of what God is saying to us remains fallible and subject to correction, that does not mean that God's word isn't genuinely at work on our hearts and minds. It just means that God has created us humans not for lives of smug sureness and unquestioning certainty, but, rather, for growth toward God precisely as creatures capable of and even haunted by questions, uncertainties, and doubts regarding the course and meaning of our life. Even if we can't know beyond all question what God is calling us to do right now, nevertheless, deep down in our bones, we know this: when we let the gospel of Jesus be brought to bear on all of life, we are growing in God's direction, for we then are growing toward the future ruled by the truth and grace of God, the future learned not by conforming ourselves to the world as it is, but by letting our lives and world be transformed by the gospel that Christ came bringing.

The work of discerning God's word, God's will, God's command, is not an exact science, and it's not about achieving absolute certainty. It's about growing to trust the path that opens up before us as we embrace the faith, hope, love, courage, and freedom that come our way through the gospel of Jesus. It's about learning to yield to his Holy Spirit's work of breaking the world's present hold on our lives and wedding us instead—heart, soul, mind, and strength—to the future that God intends, the future that Jesus called God's coming kingdom, the future that he is calling you and me, here and now, to set foot into and, here on Earth, to begin to serve.

Even and precisely in this perplexing pandemic time—even and precisely in this startling moment of social, political, economic, and religious upheaval—even and precisely amidst our present conditions of social isolation brought on by the coronavirus crisis—even and precisely amidst the present demonstrations of political protest and counterprotest in our streets—even and precisely in the face of all the questions, uncertainties, and doubts that right now mark our personal lives—even and precisely in the face of all the ambiguity, anxiety, resentment, and fear that presently fill the public arena—Christ's Holy Spirit is at work, joining us together as his church so that we ourselves might learn and, in turn, show all the world the faith, hope, love, courage, and freedom that God speaks into our lives through the gospel of Jesus—the faith, hope, love, courage, and freedom through which God joins us to the future God's graciously redeeming love intends. Our job right now, your job and mine, is this: no matter what and come what may, to stay joined together in the crucial work Christ's Holy Spirit gives. Amen.

(18)

Psalm 145:1–21   Kum ba Yah.

July 19, 2020, 7th Sunday after Pentecost

Greeting
The grace of the Lord Jesus Christ be with you all!

In and through this service of worship, we are invited to call on God by joining voice in praise and prayer, expressing our gratitude to God, invoking God's continued care, and striving to hear and heed God's word.

What we sing and say and do here, we offer up to God, for God to turn into God's way of speaking God's own word into our lives. We're here to call on God and, as we do that, to listen for the God who called us here, to send us out into the world with new eyes and ears for who we are and why we're here and what our life should be about.

God is out to speak guidance and grace into your heart and mind today. God's aim is to bless you with tasks to carry out, for the sake of God's coming kingdom. And your aim—our aim—should be this: to hear and heed God's word aright and humbly, boldly, take up our tasks.

It belongs to my prayer that this service of worship shall help us all to grow in openness for the word of the Lord—the word God spoke into the world through the history, the prophets, and the writings of Israel, the word that became incarnate in the world in the life and mission of Jesus Christ, the word that

200

Christ's Holy Spirit is breathing into our life together, even now. Amen.

✛ ✛

Announcements

For the sake of any visitors joining us today, let me note that I am Ruskin Falls, the minister here at Pulaski Heights Presbyterian Church. Joining me in our sanctuary on this Friday afternoon for the video recording of this worship service are three other members of our church family. David Harper is here as our videographer, doing his usual gracious job of helping our less-than-technologically-talented congregation take some very strong fledgling strides into the electronic age we're now in. Charles Gray, who is a member of our session, chair of our Worship Committee, and occasional Sunday school teacher, is serving as liturgist today. And Sally Todd, who is our church's music director, is at the piano to lift us into the music of worship. And let me add that I much appreciate Sally's wonderful work of keeping us musically connected in this socially distanced time.

Let me extend a reminder to all who are joining us at this time, that we send out a congregational email each week (usually on Thursday, and a real letter to those who don't do email) that includes a few words from me and also information regarding the upcoming video worship service. If you aren't on our mailing list but would like to be, just let us know, and we'll be glad to add you, be it to the email list, the real mail list, or both.

Let me also note that, last Wednesday afternoon, a number of us managed very successfully to get together electronically for our church's very first congregational Zoom gathering, and actually it was a lot of fun. I'm not sure when we'll go for a second one, but certainly we'll keep everyone posted. And, especially if we have to be a socially distanced congregation a lot longer, I hope that more and more of our members will give it a try. If you're not a member of our church but would like to Zoom with us sometime, send us your email address, and we'll be glad to send you the information you need to Zoom with us as well. We look forward to getting to know you—and letting you get to know us a little better as well.

+ +

Psalm 145:1–21   *Kum ba Yah.*

TEXT *(English translation: NRSV)*

    I will extol you, my God and King, and bless your name forever and ever. Every day I will bless you, and praise your name forever and ever. Great is the LORD, and greatly to be praised; his greatness is unsearchable.

    One generation shall laud your works to another, and shall declare your mighty acts. On the glorious splendor of your majesty, and on your wondrous works, I will meditate. The might of your awesome deeds shall be proclaimed, and I will declare your greatness. They shall celebrate the fame of your abundant goodness, and shall sing aloud of your righteousness.

    The LORD is gracious and merciful, slow to anger and abounding in steadfast love. The LORD is good to all, and his compassion is over all that he has made.

All your works shall give thanks to you, O LORD, and all your faithful shall bless you. They shall speak of the glory of your kingdom, and tell of your power, to make known to all people your mighty deeds, and the glorious splendor of your kingdom. Your kingdom is an everlasting kingdom, and your dominion endures throughout all generations.

The LORD is faithful in all his words, and gracious in all his deeds. The LORD upholds all who are falling, and raises up all who are bowed down. The eyes of all look to you, and you give them their food in due season. You open your hand, satisfying the desire of every living thing.

The LORD is just in all his ways, and kind in all his doings. The LORD is near to all who call on him, to all who call on him in truth. He fulfills the desire of all who fear him; he also hears their cry, and saves them.

The LORD watches over all who love him, but all the wicked he will destroy. My mouth will speak the praise of the LORD, and all flesh will bless his holy name forever and ever.

(1)

The Book of Psalms was ancient Israel's prayer book and hymnal. It contains prayers and songs that reflected and that nourished Israel's life as a worshiping community. These prayers and songs also reflect and nourish the life of the biblical worshiping community that you and I are, as the church of the resurrection Spirit of the child of Israel, Jesus Christ,

In the words of the psalmist, our services of divine worship are about learning *to call on God in truth*. They are about gathering before God in all God's mystery, to learn the truth that God has to teach us regarding ourselves, our world, and God. In worship, we let words and gestures inspired by biblical tradition teach us to recognize, acknowledge, and confess that we have needs and longings that the world itself cannot satisfy, but that God can and will meet us in and guide us through. Our service of worship is about lowering the volume on what the world is telling us about ourselves and about others and about God and becoming more attuned to the word that comes to us from God alone. Our service of worship is about calling on God to take what we offer—to take what we say and sing and do as a worshiping community—and to turn it into God's way of speaking God's own word into our hearts and minds and life together.

(2)

Great is the Lord, declares the psalmist, *and greatly to be praised*. On the other hand, the psalm goes on, *God's greatness is unsearchable*.

It might seem odd to call God great and yet declare God's greatness to be beyond our grasp; it might seem odd to call God great and then declare God to be so shrouded in mystery as to exceed our understanding. That sounds as if we're calling God great without knowing anything about God. Might it not turn out that God actually is a scoundrel and that we are but pawns in a game God is playing? Why call God great, if we can't actually know God?

But we *do* know God. Being unable to grasp God doesn't mean we don't know God at all. We have been given profoundly important things to know regarding God. The point, though, is this: these things are *given* to us. They aren't things that we or others discovered or reasoned out on our own. They aren't things we simply taught ourselves. Rather, they are things that God has *revealed* regarding who God is and what God is up to; they are things that God has *given* us to know regarding God, regarding our world, and regarding ourselves—things that, in turn, have opened us to paths of discovery and ways of thinking that are more than, greater than, higher than, deeper than, and, yes, more mysterious than, merely worldly paths of discovery and ways of thinking.

Among the things noted in Psalm 145 that God has revealed in the biblical community of worship are these: that God is the God of *abundant goodness and righteousness*; that God is *gracious and merciful, slow to anger, and abounding in steadfast love*; that God is *good to all* and that *God's compassion is over all that God has made*; that God is *faithful in all God's words and gracious in all God's deeds*; that God *upholds all who are falling and raises up all who are bowed down*; that God is *the God of justice and of kindness*, whose nearness we learn as we learn to *call on God in truth*, and in which nearness *God hears our cry and saves us*.

In other words, it is given to the biblical community of worship to know *God's greatness* as the God who is graciously and compassionately determined to be with us and for us to hear our cry and to save us—the God who, to all eternity, is set on turning even lives of wickedness into lives of love, till at last God's own love rules in every heart in every part of all creation.

There is, though, something about God's greatness that indeed is unsearchable, beyond our grasp, so shrouded in mystery that it exceeds our understanding. That something is this: the greatness of God's grace, mercy, love, goodness, righteousness, holiness, compassion, faithfulness, justice, kindness, and salvation—the greatness of God's determination to be with us and for us to hear our cry and to save us from whatever might threaten us with final separation from the glorious splendor of God's coming kingdom. We cannot grasp, we cannot conceive, we cannot understand how or why it is that we have been given life and are awaited at this life's end by so wondrous a God. We cannot grasp, we cannot conceive, we cannot understand our belonging to so glorious a time to come. The most that we can do is to be grateful to God and, for the time being, strive to call on God in truth—strive to call on God to turn our words and gestures of worship into God's way of speaking God's word into our hearts and minds—God's way of giving us guidance and direction.

(3)

Again, a service of worship is a prayer to God to come to us here and use what we here sing and say and do, to speak to us the word that God alone can speak—the word of grace, mercy, love, goodness, righteousness, holiness, compassion, faithfulness, justice, kindness, and salvation through which God gives us the guidance and direction God knows we need. The aim of our service of worship is to be a time and place together for *calling on God in truth*—a time and place for calling on God to be with us here to turn us into hearers and doers of God's word.

Here at Pulaski Heights Presbyterian Church, we regularly emphasize worship's aim when, just before the scripture reading and sermon, we sing together the opening verse of "Kum ba Yah."

It is typical in churches, just before the scripture reading and sermon, for an individual (usually the preacher) to offer what is called a *prayer for illumination*. A typical prayer for illumination would go something like this: "God, open our hearts and minds to your Spirit, that, as the scriptures are read and your word proclaimed, we may hear and understand your will."

The point is that simply listening to scripture read and a sermon preached can't assure that we will hear what God desires for us to hear in that moment. That happens only as the Holy Spirit works on our spirits to open us, to free us, and, so, to ready us to hear and heed God's word, God's will, God's command. With a prayer for illumination, we are praying for the presence of God's Holy Spirit working among us to do just that.

"Kum ba Yah" serves here as our prayer for illumination. It comes from an African American tradition in which, as a prayer to God, it means, "Come by here." What we are doing in singing that is this: rather than the preacher praying individually for God's presence among us as we listen for God's word, we let the congregation sing the prayer for illumination together, with a song so simple that it is widely known as a children's song, though it is a song with a profound history behind it as a prayer for God's presence, in and through a particular service of worship, especially in troubled times.

As our members know, ordinarily, when we're worshiping here in the sanctuary together, a few from among us will step up to the chancel area and sing the first verse of "Kum ba Yah" and then repeat it; as the verse is repeated, everyone else is invited to join the singing.

When, Sunday mornings, we sing "Kum ba Yah," we are praying together, in song, for God's holy presence among us, to help us hear, not necessarily the word we ourselves want to hear, and not necessarily the word the preacher may have thought we needed to hear, but, rather, the wondrously mysterious word that very God desires for us uniquely and individually to discern *through* the words of scripture read and of sermon preached.

(4)

I once was introduced to some people as the minister at Pulaski Heights Presbyterian Church. One person there who obviously knew at least a few things about our congregation remarked with what sounded to me like a sneer in his voice, "Isn't that the kumbaya church?" I thought about it and then said simply, "Yes, we are the kumbaya church."

I think I know why there was a sneer in that person's voice. It was a sneer that, actually, I hear often enough these days, in connection with "Kum ba Yah." I'm not sure how the situation has come about that calls forth that sneer, but I expect it has something to do with the fact that, over time, "Kum ba Yah" became prominent and popular as a children's church-camp song.

Imagine, for a moment, that scene: church children are gathered around the evening campfire. In the glow of the fire, as the sparks fly upward, church-camp harmony, hope, and idealism are in the air. Across whatever differences distinguish them, young people are rubbing shoulders, sharing smiles, and joining hands as if even the world that they'll be returning to at week's end can be filled with the peace and love and understanding that a week at church camp tends to foster. And they begin singing, *Kum ba yah, my Lord, kum ba yah!...Someone's crying, Lord, kum ba yah!...Someone's singing, Lord, kum ba yah...Someone's praying, Lord, kum ba yah!...O Lord, kum ba yah!*

Nowadays, that is the familiar setting for the singing of "Kum ba Yah." And many grown-ups—tempered, hardened, and maybe also calloused by what we call "real life"—have, in turn, come to associate "Kum ba Yah" with a childish idealism, a naive optimism, and simplistically warm and cozy feelings that, the grown-ups insist, will never survive or even be effective in the real world, made up, as the real world is, of competition and conflict, rivalry and hostility, self-assertive will-to-power and combative survival of the fittest, the strongest, and the cleverest.

I think it important that we set the record straight.

This song comes to us from the Gullah people. The Gullah live on islands along the southeastern coast of United States. Their ancestors came from the rice-growing regions of West Africa. They were brought to America as slaves to cultivate rice plantations on those American coastal islands.

Here is what Columbia University professor Samuel Freedman wrote regarding the earliest known recording of "Kum ba Yah," made in 1926: "Kum ba Yah" tells "of people in despair and in trouble, calling on heaven for help, and beseeching God in the refrain, 'Come by here.'" It is "a song deeply rooted in Black Christianity's vision of a God who intercedes to deliver both solace and justice." In its original hands, it "appealed for divine intervention on behalf of the oppressed. The people who were 'crying, my Lord' were Blacks suffering under the Jim Crow regime of lynch mobs and sharecropping."[12]

"Kum ba Yah" was sung as the cry of those who know they need God's presence with them in this oh-so wonderful and yet oh-so conflicted world, to give them the guidance and direction—to give them the wisdom, peace, and courage—that they need and that comes only from God.

When we sing "Kum ba Yah," we are calling on God in truth. We are calling on God to come to us here. We are calling on God to come to us amidst all our hopes and needs, all our joy and gladness, all our pain and suffering, and to use what we here sing and say and do, to speak to us the word that God and God alone can speak, the word through which God gives us the guidance and direction that God knows we most deeply need here and now, for the sake of the future that God intends.

"Kum ba Yah" actually is an importantly realistic song that every child of the church, of every age, needs to learn prayerfully and oft to sing, particularly when gathered for worship, and especially in troubled times. And I would hope that, in the future, should anyone ask of any of our members—even if with a sneer—"Aren't y'all the kumbaya church?" you will reply joyfully seriously, "Yes, we are the kumbaya church," and then give thanks and praise to God—the God whose greatness is unsearchable and yet who has touched our hearts and minds and lives as the God of abundant goodness and righteousness; who is gracious and merciful, slow to anger, and abounding in steadfast love; who is good to all and whose compassion is over

---

[12] Samuel Friedman, *New York Times* (November 19, 2010).

all that God has made; who is faithful in all God's words and gracious in all God's deeds; who upholds all who are falling and raises up all who are bowed down; who is the God of justice and of kindness, whose nearness we learn as we learn to call on God in truth; and who, amidst all the mystery of God's ways, hears our cry and saves us. Amen.

19

Ephesians 4:17–24   The new self.

July 26, 2020, 8th Sunday after Pentecost

Greeting
The grace of the Lord Jesus Christ be with you all!

Worship is about learning to feel God's passionate and compassionate love for the world. Worship is about learning to think, not merely from a center in ourselves, but from a center that is in God. Worship is about learning to do God's goodness justice in this world.

It belongs to my prayer that, through this time of worship, we may learn more profoundly to sense—and become better readied to carry out—the tasks that God has entrusted to us for the sake of the future that God is calling into being. May this service of worship be for us a constant prayer to God for strength and courage in all that we do as the covenant community of the Holy Spirit of Jesus Christ our Lord. Amen.

+ +

Announcements
I'm Ruskin Falls, the minister here at Pulaski Heights Presbyterian Church. Joining me in our sanctuary to record this worship service for our congregation are three other members of our church family. David Harper is standing amongst the

pews amidst a tangle of cables operating our audio and video equipment. Sally Todd is at the piano to lift us into the music of worship. And LaWanda Harris is with me in the chancel area to serve as our liturgist.

Next Sunday, August 2, LaWanda will be doing the preaching for our worship service. Our church's session has given me some time off next week, and we once again have called on LaWanda to step in to provide worship leadership and preaching in my stead. We're asking her to do this on top of her work as a hospice nurse here in Little Rock, and on top of her work as a student in the distance program of the University of Dubuque Theological Seminary, through which she herself is preparing to enter the ordained ministry of the Presbyterian Church (U.S.A.). I am grateful for LaWanda's readiness, willingness, and ability to juggle so well at the same time the many important and demanding responsibilities that she has taken on.

So LaWanda will be filling the pulpit next Sunday, August 2. And I'll be returning to the pulpit the following Sunday, August 9.

It is to be anticipated that our congregation is going to be worshiping together for a time to come via this online-only platform. Our session has not set a date for returning to in-person gatherings in our building. Given the ominous course that COVID-19 still appears to be on in Arkansas generally and especially in central Arkansas, we think it best for now for our particular congregation to continue seeking ways of staying in touch and carrying out the work of the church otherwise than physically hand-in-hand, shoulder-to-shoulder, and face-to-face.

I daresay we've been doing this longer now than we were thinking of having to do it when we halted in-person gatherings back in March. At this point we indeed have entered unchartered territory regarding how, in circumstances of forced absence, to carry out the tasks and responsibilities of the church—how to be the church our members need right now, and how to be the church that the world (whether it realizes it or not!) is in need of right now. It isn't clear just how we are to keep on keeping on for who knows how long, staying physically distanced enough to keep each other virus-free while nevertheless carrying out what we Presbyterians call "The great ends of the Church," which are these:

the proclamation of the gospel for the salvation of humankind;
the shelter, nurture, and spiritual fellowship of the children of God;
the maintenance of divine worship;
the preservation of the truth;
the promotion of social righteousness; and
the exhibition of the Kingdom of Heaven to the world.
(*Book of Order, F-1.0304*)

Again: It is not clear just where the road ahead is leading us. What *is* clear is that the path the church now is on in this country is winding its way through a world filled with hurt—hurt in the form of the physical, emotional, and economic suffering that has come our way through the coronavirus and the public policies that had to be employed to avoid the still greater harm this virus has the potential to cause, and hurt in the form of the physical, emotional, and economic suffering that has been inflicted on many in our society by the way others of us have allowed our racial prejudice, class privilege, ease of access to political power, and dominance over economic resources, to—sometimes blatantly, sometimes subtly, sometimes even unconsciously—run roughshod over more democratic inclinations, institutions, and ways of being a nation.

The church doesn't have a plan for solving all these woes. In fact, all too often, large and influential portions of the church itself have belonged more to the problem than to the solution. Moreover, however, even at our Christian best, we do not have from Jesus a concrete social, political, or economic program that is the solution to all these woes. What Jesus does give us, though, are these: the orientation we need, the direction we need, the guidance, grace, and love we need, if we indeed are to live in ways that make our world more like the world that God intends.

+ +

Ephesians 4:17–24 *The new self.*

TEXT *(English translation: NRSV)*

> Now this I affirm and insist on in the Lord: you must no longer live as the Gentiles live, in the futility of their minds. They are darkened in their understanding, alienated from the life of God because of their ignorance and hardness of heart. They have lost all sensitivity and have abandoned themselves to licentiousness, greedy to practice every kind of impurity. That is not the way you learned Christ! For surely you have heard about him and were taught in him, as truth is in Jesus. You were

taught to put away your former way of life, your old self, corrupt and deluded by its lusts, and to be renewed in the spirit of your minds, and to clothe yourselves with the new self, created according to the likeness of God in true righteousness and holiness.

(1)

Through Jesus Christ we meet with the new self that God desires for us to clothe ourselves with. Jesus lived on Earth according to the likeness of God, in true righteousness and holiness. In him is the truth that God intends for us to know regarding who we are and how we should live. In him is the truth that conforms our self and our life to God's good will and way. It is as you and I study, learn from, and come to know Jesus, and it is as we let our lives be changed by how he lived, that we can put away our old self and clothe ourselves with the new self that is in keeping with the loving righteousness, the gracious holiness, and the infinite goodness of God.

I want now to sketch a picture of this Jesus who lived according to the likeness of God and whom we are to let ourselves be changed by.

Admittedly, no one's picture of Jesus is beyond being improved on and corrected. Even a picture well-grounded in scripture is a picture that is tinted by one's way of interpreting scripture. And the very fact that there are differing ways of interpreting scripture makes for differences in the respective pictures of Jesus that people draw. Moreover, there are always new things to be learned regarding Jesus. New insights and new perspectives are gained as your faith matures, as you study the Bible harder, and as new experiences come your way. And these things can be expected to call forth changes in your picture of Jesus. So, the picture I'm offering is one among other possible pictures. Neither this picture of Jesus nor anyone else's is beyond needing to be updated through further study and through exposure to new experiences and perspectives. We do need to keep in mind that knowledge of Jesus is something we work toward and grow into by remaining always open to learning something new.

The picture of Jesus I'm about to draw is not original with me. It's the one that was drawn by the Swiss theologian, Karl Barth.[13] I see in Barth's picture a compelling interpretation of what the Bible gives us to see and hear and acknowledge regarding Jesus's life. And today I want to point you toward that picture, beginning with this question: Just how did he live, this Jesus who lived on Earth according to the likeness of God?

(2)

For starters, he lived amidst and suffered under much *humiliation*.

Jesus was born poor, and he died by execution as a criminal. His life was lacking in worldly glamor, honor, and achievement. Many took offense at things he said and did. His own townspeople regarded him skeptically and discounted his worth. Some of his own relatives suspected him of being somewhere between disturbingly eccentric and outright crazy. He was criticized by many people for being unduly festive with persons of dubious character. He owned nothing and had, as he

---

[13] Karl Barth, *Church Dogmatics* (Edinburgh: T. & T. Clark, 1958), 166-192.

himself put it, no place to lay his head. He was dependent on the hospitality and charity of others to meet his needs.

Temple leaders looked down on him as a shameless blasphemer; palace authorities looked down on him as a rebellious troublemaker; and the soldiers who crucified him heaped derision on him in his final hours. Of course, humiliation was one of the *aims* of a crucifixion. Crucifixion forced a person to die excruciatingly slowly on public display, being scoffed at by onlookers and picked on by scavenger birds and insects. Victims died agonized, bloody, filthy, and naked (later paintings of Jesus to the contrary, there were no towels around the waist of a criminal on a cross!). Even worse, Jesus's own would-be followers—those he called his "disciples"—were constantly uncertain what to make of him, unsure how to understand him, and, in the end, unready to stand by him. They betrayed, denied, and abandoned Jesus and his cause.

In a word: Jesus lived and Jesus died humiliated by the world around him.

(3)

Also, Jesus demonstrated a *preference* for the company of people who themselves had had experience with humiliation.

When we look at the kinds of people he generally chose to spend time with, it's as if he had a bias in favor of the weak, the meek, and the lowly, over against the socially influential, the politically powerful, and the materially comfortable. And note well, it was not the great urban centers that Jesus chose as locations for his work, but rather the small, poverty-stricken villages along the dusty back roads of Galilee. Moreover, he tended to ignore those widely regarded as morally upright, in favor of the company of people looked down on and scorned as uncouth sinners whose proximity good taste cannot stand. Also, he outraged fellow Jews by crossing racial lines and embracing the company of non-Jews.

In a word: Jesus took this world's way of measuring greatness and insignificance, weakness and strength, beauty and ugliness, sickness and health, morality and immorality, and he stood it on its head by constantly embracing precisely the sat-upon and the spat-upon of this world, the scorned and the broken, the detested and the despised, the humiliated.

(4)

Finally, even amidst his own and others' humiliating circumstances, Jesus displayed a remarkable *freedom* both in relation to the reigning order of things and in relation to existing movements set on changing the order of things.

Jesus did consistently take the side of those who were being crushed by the world as it is. Yet, he was not a reformer working to replace the old order with a new one through some social, political, economic, moral, or religious program. He did not identify himself with any particular party. He did not set up his own party in competition with the others. He identified himself neither with the existing order nor with any of the reform movements of his day, such as the Pharisees, the Essenes, that of John the Baptizer, or others. He treated all worldly orders, both the existing order and all programs set on reforming the existing order, as severely limited in what they actually accomplish. He treated them as conditioned by human habit in ways that render them all inevitably fallible and flawed. He treated them as strictly relative and only provisional. Also, he was regarded with equal suspicion and disapproval by the representatives of the existing order and by the representatives of the reform movements. He treated no particular way of ordering society as absolutely necessary, and he clashed with all existing or proposed ways of ordering society. Still, he did not work to overthrow, replace, or amend any of them. Curiously, in fact, Jesus accepted or at least tolerated some traditional social values and institutions that we today might think he should have attacked and worked to set aside.

Jesus showed respect for the traditional order of the family. He even emphasized caring for one's parents as being of greater importance than tending to otherwise important religious duties. Nevertheless, he did show great respect for the temple. He took it seriously as the house of God and taught others to do the same. He refused to separate himself from the temple, even though the persons who controlled it—the Sadducees—were some of the very folks most responsible for the social oppression Jesus wanted to free people from.

Nor did Jesus separate himself from the Galilean synagogues and their traditionalism regarding religious law. He even emphasized that he had come not to destroy but to fulfill the law, and he talked about the importance of even seemingly minute religious regulations.

Nor did Jesus come into direct conflict with the economic relationships and obligations of his time. For example, he talked about masters and slaves without stopping to criticize the practice of slavery, and he talked about the poor as if there always would be people who were poor.

Nor did Jesus, prior to his final week, come into direct conflict with agencies of political law and order. Though he denounced the present order as corrupt, he talked about courts, prisons, and executive powers without further criticism. He talked about some tyrants without insisting on their overthrow, and he spoke of one despotic governor as if that tyrant should be obeyed. And while there's ample evidence of Jesus's disdain for Roman imperialism and militarism, he was known to befriend Roman soldiers, and he endorsed no party's plan for overthrowing Rome.

In a word: Jesus lived out a kind of passive conservatism. He acknowledged, reckoned with, and subjected himself to the existing order of things. And he advised disciples to do the same.

However, that doesn't mean he gave his endorsement to the present order of things. Again, Jesus treated everything about the existing order as limited, relative, fallible, flawed, and merely provisional. At the heart of his mission was his proclamation that the kingdom of God had come among us, and that that kingdom was *utterly different from, radically opposed to,* and *infinitely better than* any and all our human ways of ordering the world.

For example, as regards the temple, he insisted that it was not an absolutely good thing, and that there was something in what Jesus himself was up to, that was far greater than the temple.

As regards family, Jesus often assaulted traditional family values. He said his real family was not those whom society recognized as his family, but rather those who heard and heeded his word. When a man who wanted to become Jesus's disciple wanted first to go bid his family farewell, Jesus told him, in effect, to forget his family and concentrate on the work that Jesus was giving him to do. Another who wanted to be his disciple asked to be allowed first to go bury his deceased father, and Jesus told the man he couldn't both be a disciple and keep to a traditional focus on the family. Far from promoting traditional family values, Jesus counseled that becoming his disciple would stress and strain and sometimes even break one's family ties.

As regards religious law, Jesus openly breached prevailing religious traditions and customs. He and his disciples were regularly criticized for neglecting prescribed rituals and sacrifices. Time and again, they offended people by violating the rules for ritual cleanliness and purity, and by violating the law regarding Sabbath observance. Jesus talked about the kingdom of God as being more sublime than any laws, more sublime even than the law of the Sabbath.

As regards the economic order, particularly in his parables and in his daily living, Jesus insisted that single-minded focus on serving God's coming kingdom is infinitely superior to the self-serving pursuit of worldly gain and profit.

The same holds with respect to political law and order. Time and again, Jesus insisted that wholehearted loyalty to God's coming kingdom is infinitely more important than is loyalty to any worldly kingdom, empire, nation, government, regime, or administration.

Such acts and attitudes as these got Jesus into serious trouble with persons of influence and power. In the end, it got him crucified. Yet, in an important sense, Jesus did not do battle with the ways of the world. He didn't declare a crusade against ungodly ways of organizing life and society. He didn't join any one party's program in opposition to other parties' programs. But, he did proclaim and serve the coming of the kingdom of the God of grace and love as something that already was making itself known and effective in and through Jesus's own life and mission. And he declared God's coming kingdom to be better than and superior to all the ways we humans have found for ordering human life and society. He declared that, in the light of God's coming kingdom, the present world— even at its most concerned and caring best!—turns out to be demonically dominated by sin, demonically dominated by attitudes, postures, and ways that are at odds with God. And Jesus's words and actions got him killed—executed—crucified. There is evil at work throughout our world, and Jesus opposed it. And yet he did not so much strike evil down as let himself be struck down *by* the very evil whose overcoming was his aim.

In a word, Jesus talked and lived as if the kingdom of God that is manifesting itself in the world through him, manifests itself in opposition to and as a challenge to our present ways of ordering human life—be they the way of traditional values or the way of changing values, be they the ways of the old regime or be they programs for reform. There is, says Jesus, something about all human ways of organizing and ordering life, that actually offends God. And it is by daring to take up the challenging cause of God's coming kingdom, that we do God's goodness justice.

(5)

That, I would suggest, is a soundly biblical picture of the Jesus in whom we meet God's truth regarding who we are and how we should live. This Jesus focuses us on and admonishes and challenges us with such questions as: How can we live *in* without being merely *of* this world? How can we relish life and enjoy this world that God intends to be relished and enjoyed, without distancing ourselves from God's good will and way, and without falling into resistance to God? How can we cherish life as a blessing and gift from God, now that we've turned the world into and, for so, so long, tolerated it as a place tragically at odds with the world that God intends?

And the answer? Grow to know Jesus; let yourself be changed by how he lived; and take up the cause of God's coming kingdom, daring, in a world of sin, to do God's goodness justice. Amen.

20

1ˢᵗ John 4:7–16   The love God is.

August 9, 2020, 10ᵗʰ Sunday after Pentecost

Greeting
The grace of the Lord Jesus Christ be with you all!

It belongs to God's promise to us, to take what we say and sing and do in divine worship and use that to speak God's own word to us.

There are things you need that the world can't give you and that you can't give yourself. There are things you need that only God can put into your heart, into your mind, into your spirit, into action in your life. Through things said and sung and done in our service of worship, we are to listen for God's own guidance and grace coming uniquely into each of our lives, alerting us to how far from God we've fallen, awakening us to God's redeeming love, and emboldening us to do what needs to be done to make this world more like the world that God intends through the gospel of Jesus.

It belongs to my prayer that this service of worship may serve well what God is up to with us today. Amen.

+ +

Announcements
For the sake of visitors joining us for this worship service, let me note that my name is Ruskin Falls. I serve as minister here

225

at Pulaski Heights Presbyterian Church, and I'll be doing the preaching today. Joining me in our sanctuary to record this worship service are three other members of our church family. David Harper is operating our audio/video equipment. Sally Todd is at the piano to lift us into the music of worship. And LaWanda Harris is here in the chancel to serve as our liturgist.

I want to extend a word of thanks to LaWanda for filling the pulpit here last Sunday in my absence. LaWanda has one more year to go in the distance program of the University of Dubuque Theological Seminary. She'll then receive her Master of Divinity degree, which degree is one of the requirements for entering the ordained ministry of the Presbyterian Church (U.S.A.).

Let me mention just one of the things that has impressed me as I have observed LaWanda's growth into her ministerial calling: LaWanda approaches her seminary studies and her congregational responsibilities both with dead serious diligence and with a lively sense of humor that keeps her mindful that we ministers need always to guard against taking ourselves unduly seriously, and that we need always to strive to take with utmost seriousness the word that God has spoken and speaks into the world through the history of Jesus Christ— which history includes God's formation of the people of Israel as the community in which Christ's life and mission had its roots and was given instruction and direction, and which history includes the working of God's Holy Spirit among us even now in Christ's church. It is not ourselves but God's word that we are to take supremely seriously—and more seriously even than life and death. For it is in and through God's word that we meet with the guidance and grace that we most deeply need, if we are to go about our daily life, navigate its trials and tribulations, and prepare for our approaching death with the kind of courage and delight—and sense of humor—that we were lovingly created to know and to grow into over the long haul.

Of course, taking God's word seriously involves taking the worship of God seriously. And divine worship is a communal experience. Even our times of private devotion and meditation are ultimately grounded in experiences of the worshiping community. And one of the questions that we so abruptly crashed into back in March was this: what does it mean to be a worshiping community in the time of Covid-19?

On March 21, our session made the decision that, for the time being, it meant finding a way to do that without in-person congregational gatherings. And, despite being, I'm sure, one of Little Rock's more low-tech churches, we decided to begin—on March 29—providing video services over our website. Our aim right now is to continue offering video services even after we return to in-person services, and to, in fact, return to in-person services as soon as we deem that the faithful, wise, and caring thing for our particular congregation to do. The next stated meeting of the session (not in person but via Zoom) will be held following worship next Sunday. We'll take stock of our situation at that point and try responsibly to wrap our hearts and minds around the questions: how much longer must we wait? And, when the time is right, what would make good sense as a faithful, fitting, and responsible *way* of reopening our doors to in-person worship?

If you have thoughts, concerns, and insights to share in this regard, please do that by contacting me or any other of our session members or by contacting the church office. And I will keep you posted regarding where next Sunday's session meeting leads.

+ +

1st John 4:7–16   *The love God is.*

TEXT *(English translation: NRSV)*

Beloved, let us love one another, because love is from God; everyone who loves is born of God and knows God. Whoever does not love does not know God, for God is love. God's love was revealed among us in this way: God sent his only Son into the world so that we might live through him. In this is love, not that we loved God but that he loved us and sent his Son to be the atoning sacrifice for our sins. Beloved, since God loved us so much, we also ought to love one another. No one has ever seen God; if we love one another, God lives in us, and his love is perfected in us.

By this we know that we abide in him and he in us, because he has given us of his Spirit. And we have seen and do testify that the Father has sent his Son as the Savior of the world. God abides in those who confess that Jesus is the Son of God, and they abide in God. So we have known and believe the love that God has for us.

God is love, and those who abide in love abide in God, and God abides in them.

(1)

God is love.

In a brief and insightful introduction to the letters of John, Presbyterian minister and New Testament scholar Lewie Donelson rightly notes that that says more than just that God loves us. It says more than just that God is loving. It says more than just that love is one part of God's character. Rather, it says that God *is* love. It declares that God cannot be detached from love or love from God. Moreover, if God is love, then everything about God has to do with love. In saying God is love, we're saying that "God can do many things, but all of them must be aspects of love. Thus even if we can say that God judges or punishes, we can only say those things if judging and punishing belong to love." Even the likes of divine punishment or divine judgment can have nothing to do with desire on God's part to cause us harm or get even with us for some wrong. Even should God discipline us, it can only be by letting love bring out in us what is best about us—letting love bring out in us what fits us for the future God's love intends. Nothing that God ever does will be contrary to the love God is.[14]

(2)

That God is love doesn't necessarily mean that God is what the world has taught you and me to call "love." The world has taught us many ways of using the word love. We have reason to talk of love in the context of romance, eroticism, patriotism,

[14] Lewis R. Donelson, *From Hebrews to Revelation: A Theological Introduction* (Louisville: Westminster John Knox Press, 2001), 107.

enjoyment, affection, friendship, family, and so on. We go wrong, however, when we presume that being able to use the word love in such contexts as these means we know what we're saying when we say, "God is love." The reason is this: what we know of God we know, not because we, with all our worldly research tools, have discovered, identified, and analyzed God, but rather because God has done what we cannot conceive: oh-so mysteriously, in the life and mission of Jesus, *God* has *broken into*, God has *interrupted*, our worldly lives to lift us into otherworldly God's own life. In the Jesus Christ who was born of Mary, crucified during the reign of Pontius Pilate, and then returned to his disciples as the resurrected one—in the life and mission of this Jesus, invisible God has taken up residence in our visible world; eternal God has set up shop in our passing world; wholly other God has entered our human world as one who meets us face-to-face, rubs shoulders with us, sits at table with us, and speaks to us. In Jesus Christ God teaches us that God is, who God is, and God's way with the world.

In Jesus Christ.

That is to say: the Jesus Christ who was born to Mary and Joseph of Nazareth in Galilee under the military rule of the Roman Empire in the time of Herod the Great; who suffered under and was crucified during the Roman rule of Pontius Pilate; who was returned as the resurrected one to the very disciples who, before his death, had betrayed, denied, and abandoned him; and who, as the resurrected one, began opening people to God as they had never before been open, as the God of genuine love.

The disciples came away from their experiences of the resurrected Jesus in the amazed conviction that God is the love that suffered and died for the sake of a godless world, the love that is eternally set on saving precisely that world. Theologian Austin Farrer describes nicely this conviction the disciples were left with regarding God: "What, then, did God do for his people's redemption? He came among them, bringing his kingdom, and he let events take their human course. He set the divine life in human neighbourhood. Men discovered it in struggling with it and were captured by it in crucifying it. What could be simpler? And what more divine?"[15]

(3)

Consider for a moment the biblical Nativity Story and the scene of Jesus's birth. Not a shiny palace, but a drafty barn. Not surrounded by the trappings of royalty, but watched over by lowly Mary and Joseph, two poverty- and scandal-ridden Jews in the little nowhere town of Bethlehem amidst the mighty and, for Jews, onerous and oppressive Roman Empire. And there is no fairy-tale ending to this story. As Matthew tells it, Joseph and Mary found themselves, in the end, forced to flee Jesus's birthplace in Bethlehem and journey to Egypt with their child in order to keep him from being killed by imperial soldiers. To save Jesus, they became, for a while, jobless immigrants in a foreign land.

Also, Jesus's adult life was filled with rejection, humiliation, agony, and suffering. And he died a tortured death, deserted, scorned, humiliated, and ridiculed by those around him. And, after his death and even after his resurrection, the world

---

[15] Austin Farrer, *Saving Belief: A Discussion of Essentials* (London: Hodder and Stoughton, 1964), 99.

still looked pretty much just like the sinful world it had been before, up to its ears in subjection to principalities and powers opposed to God's loving will for the world—up to its ears in subjection to forces and ways of domination and violence, greed and resentment, meanness and contempt, arrogance and corruption, humiliation and condemnation, poverty and destitution, demoralization and despair, illness and injury, fear and death—forces and ways of being that are perniciously and horribly opposed to the future God's love intends.

The coming of God's love in the life and mission of Jesus did not magically change people's worldly circumstances. It didn't end anyone's poverty. It didn't ease anyone's hardships. It didn't liberate anyone from Roman oppression. It didn't end the arbitrary and cruel rule of King Herod or prevent the arbitrary and cruel rule of Pontius Pilate.

It could have happened otherwise, but it didn't. Almighty God could have come among us in a show of force, sweeping away in one fell swoop all the principalities and powers that exist in opposition to the world that God intends—sweeping away in one fell swoop sin's ways of burdening our world with so much foolishness, sadness, injustice, and suffering. But God did not do that. That is not the way of God's love, not the way of the love God is, not the way—we now know—of genuine love.

While genuine love desires a genuinely loving world, a genuinely loving world cannot be coerced into being. Genuine love is not something that can be forced onto others. Rather, genuine love can only be inspired and encouraged in others. Genuine love can only be, little by little, taught and learned.

In its desire for a genuinely loving world, genuine love will press for changes. Often enough, genuine love will see that others need to change into something that they, at first, weren't ready, willing, or able to become. And genuine love will work to bring them to change. Sometimes genuine love even has to be tough love. Sometimes it has to say no to loved ones in order to change them. Nevertheless, the great desire of genuine love is a genuinely loving world, and the world cannot be forced to be genuinely loving. People can only be inspired, encouraged, and, little by little, taught to be genuinely loving, through someone else's genuine love. Jesus is the genuine love of God come among us, not to force us, but to inspire and encourage and teach us to become genuinely loving.

Note well one important consequence of that: If God's primary aim is to inspire and encourage and teach us to be genuinely loving, then God's primary aim with us in this world is not to free us from all hardship, trial, and suffering. Indeed, where there is genuine love, there is going to be suffering. If you learn genuine love, you're going to suffer; you're going to hurt. For genuine love involves empathizing with others when they suffer. It involves growing to feel the pain and needs and troubles and worries and woes of others in the depths of your own soul. Genuine love is not about feeling sorry for others. It's about feeling their suffering, their troubled heart, their worried mind, their lowliness, as your own.

And, genuine love is always vulnerable. It runs the risk of being scorned and rejected by those you love. It means risking your own heart's breaking when they disappoint you or hurt you or laugh at you or are taken away from you. It involves being drawn into difficult sacrifices you otherwise would not have made and making hard choices that may leave you questioning yourself.

Moreover, genuine love means doing all that in cheerfully glad anticipation that, whatever love's agonies, setbacks, and defeats today, the day is coming when this old world shall really, truly, undoubtedly, and fully abide in God's own gloriously genuine love.

(4)

The life and mission of Jesus, from the scene of his birth, to the scene of his death, to the scenes of his resurrection appearances, is otherworldly God at work in the world declaring that God is love, showing us the nature of genuine love, and speaking genuine love into our lives. The life and mission of Jesus is the love that God *is*, coming among us and risking injury, rejection, disappointment, and defeat at human hands, in order to inspire and encourage and teach us and our world to become genuinely loving. The life and mission of Jesus shows and tells us God's loving determination not to rule us by controlling us from some throne on high, but to rule us from the manger and the cross, and through the compassionate humility, of Jesus Christ. The life and mission of Jesus is God's act of inviting us to discover in genuine love, something that is more worthy of our commitment and trust—something that is more worth risking ourselves for!—than is any merely worldly form of power or possession. The life and mission of Jesus is otherworldly God at work in the world, inspiring, encouraging, and teaching us to see and understand that genuinely loving others and becoming a genuinely loving world really and truly is what we were created to dare to do in the brief but, oh-so precious time that's been given us on this Earth. The life and mission of Jesus is God's act of showing us that genuine love—despite how much it

sometimes hurts, and despite how hard it sometimes seems—
is the divinely good and wondrous purpose of your life and
of mine.

(5)

I admit that I cannot imagine how genuine love ever finally
is going to turn our world into the world that God intends.
I have a hard time understanding how genuine love might
actually change more than just a few nearby hearts—or change
even those hearts for more than just a very limited time. It is
especially hard to see how genuine love really can dismantle
the more systemic, structural, institutional, cultural, and
societal ways in which prejudice, resentment, hatred, and fear
have wrapped themselves around and woven themselves into
our hearts and minds and lives and communities. It is hard to
see how genuine love can be expected to be a genuine match
for the ungodly forces of domination and violence, greed and
resentment, meanness and contempt, arrogance and corruption,
humiliation and condemnation, poverty and destitution,
demoralization and despair, illness and injury, fear and death,
that so perniciously and so horribly haunt our present world.

Nevertheless, the life and mission of Jesus, the biblical
witness to the word of God that he embodied, and the
movement of his resurrection Spirit among us in the church
today do wrap around me and weave into my heart and mind
and life—and, I pray, around you and into your heart and mind
and life—the amazed conviction that we were created by and
for genuine love.

And, in that amazed conviction, our calling now is this: to
let that conviction inspire and instill in us the humility and the

courage that we need to serve the justice and peace to come—the justice and peace that Jesus called God's coming kingdom—a kingdom that is rooted in genuine love; a kingdom that is the flowering of the life that genuine love desires for us all to know, enjoy, and share.

Truly, those who abide in that love abide in God. Amen.

(21)

Philippians 2:1–5   The love we can become.

August 16, 2020, 11th Sunday after Pentecost

Greeting
The grace of the Lord Jesus Christ be with you all!

Through Jesus Christ, we meet with things eternal God desires for us to know regarding forgiveness for our waywardness, graciousness in the face of our limitations, justice in the face of wrong, courage and peace in the face of violence, and love which truly nurtures and genuinely renews us. We have good reason to celebrate and rejoice in what God is up to with us through the life and mission of Jesus. Indeed, we have good reason to look reverently in this hour to the God Christ came to reveal, and to follow, in the days ahead, where God in Christ is leading.

It belongs to my prayer that the Holy Spirit will use this service of worship to speak into each of our lives the unique word of guidance and grace that God, better than we ourselves, knows we need to hear this day. Amen.

+ +

Announcements
For the sake of visitors joining us for this service, let me note that gathered here in the sanctuary of this church are four

237

members of our church family. The video equipment is being
operated by church member and church sexton David Harper.
At the piano is church member and music director Sally Todd.
Serving as liturgist is church member and seminarian LaWanda
Harris. And I'm Ruskin Falls, a member of the Presbytery of
Arkansas and the minister here at Pulaski Heights Presbyterian.
I'll be preaching today.

I will say I look forward to the day when we again can have
worshipers sitting in the pews where, right now, there stands but
a tripod with a camera on it. I look forward to the day when we
can go back to passing the peace in worship face to face and hand
in hand. I look forward to the day when we can be here with
our choir gathered before us, singing and leading us in singing.
I look forward to the day when we can share the bread and the
cup of the Lord's Supper together shoulder to shoulder in this
place. I look forward to the day when our adult Sunday school
class can gather again around the discussion table and go back
to digging into the deep and wide array of theological subjects
it's known for probing and discussing and sometimes agreeing
about and sometimes disagreeing about but always with love.
I look forward to the day when we all can sit together again and
share a potluck fellowship meal. I look forward to the day when
I can visit you in your home and have you visit me without masks,
without measured distance between us, without worrying about
possibly infecting one another with the coronavirus, and without
constantly having to remind ourselves not to hug. I look forward
to that day. And it will come. And it will be a glad occasion.

But, as that occasion has not yet arrived, we're keeping on
keeping on, doing our best to make the best of the situation
we're in with the resources that we have. I do hope that you are

finding in our online worship services a helpful and important way of listening for God's word coming your way and speaking itself into your heart and mind and life. I do long for the day when there'll be more than just a camera for me to look to from this pulpit. In the meantime, though—and despite all I ever said about never becoming a YouTube preacher!—I'm grateful that we are able to provide this opportunity for joining together at a distance for divine worship.

+ +

Philippians 2:1–5   *The love we can become.*

TEXT *(English translation: NRSV)*

> If then there is any encouragement in Christ, any consolation from love, any sharing in the Spirit, any compassion and sympathy, make my joy complete: be of the same mind, having the same love, being in full accord and of one mind. Do nothing from selfish ambition or conceit, but in humility regard others as better than yourselves. Let each of you look not to your own interests, but to the interests of others. Let the same mind be in you that was in Christ Jesus.

(1)

You are to have the same mind as Jesus. And that means you are to have the same love as Jesus. And that means not acting out of selfish ambition or conceit, but, rather, humbly regarding others as better than yourself, looking not to your own interests, but to theirs.

That's what the apostle Paul, together with his traveling companion Timothy, wrote to the Christians in Philippi. And yet, in the New Testament gospel portrayals of Jesus, his love was not devoid of desires, aspirations, and hopes of his own; his love led him to do things that challenged many people and that clearly did not yield to others as if he were inferior to them; and his love was related to interests he had that he believed it important and good to further, even if that meant contesting the interests and agendas of the people around him.

Let us therefore put the question this way: when we do look to the gospel portrayals of Jesus, in what sense is Jesus's love a love that looks unselfishly to others, humbly regarding them as better than himself, and looking to their interests rather than his own?

(2)

In the face of that question, I have found an observation made by Presbyterian minister and theologian Ed Farley to be helpful. Himself citing the work of another theologian, W.H. Vanstone, Farley offers an insightful one-line description of what he calls "genuine love" that I believe describes the kind of love that Paul sees in Jesus and that Paul is calling all Christians to embrace. Farley puts it this way: genuine love is oriented simply to other people's capacity to receive it, and genuine love strives always to enlarge their capacity to receive it.[16]

Our love for other people most often involves loving things about them that make us feel good. Such love for another can

---

[16] Edward Farley, *Divine Empathy: A Theology of God* (Minneapolis: Augsburg/Fortress, 1996), 277.

run deep, and it can move us to actions done not for our own good, but for the good of the one we love. This form of love can be profoundly important. Still, because, in this case, my love for the other person is a reaction to the good I receive from that person, it is a love that, at best, is a mixture of selfish and unselfish motives. It's a love in which I keep at least one eye on my own interests. It's a love that requires a kind of equalization between the love I give and the good I get. In order to sustain such love, I need something for myself from the other person that makes me feel good.

Jesus's love is different from that. Jesus's love for you is not focused on anything that you have given Jesus or that he otherwise gets from you that makes him feel good. Rather, his love regards you as having an immediate claim on him that he forthwith sets out to answer to, without needing anything from you either in advance or in return. He sees in you a claim on him that has priority over all his momentary desires and needs.

It might help us better understand Jesus's love if we think for a moment about the kind of love a parent has—or at least sometimes can have—for a child. (And let me note that there are also other categories of people we could look to for help in understanding Jesus's love. We could think about schoolteachers, for example, and the love that can and, in so many cases, does guide their work. For now, though, I'll stick with the example of parents.)

Admittedly, parents' love for their children does regularly get entangled in needs and longings that the parents have, that they are working out, in and through their children. Sometimes parents expect or demand things of a child, not because that particular expectation or demand truly serves the good of the child, but because the parents have issues and needs of their own that they are pushing off onto their children and working out through their children.

Nevertheless, in the relationship between parents and children—not always, but sometimes—there are glimpses of a different kind of love. There are at least occasional glimpses of a love that does not depend on having gotten something from the child, a love that is not rooted in any egoistic ambitions of the parent, a love that is there independently of what the parent receives in return. There can occur, in parental love, glimpses of a love that simply experiences the child as having the capacity to receive love and that responds forthwith to that capacity as a claim on the parent that is mysteriously more important than all the parent's own momentary needs and expectations. In the relationship between parents and children, there sometimes occur glimpses of a love that is moved not by personal ambition, conceit, or self-interest, but simply by the experience of the child's capacity to receive love and the immediate urge to do things that will enlarge that capacity. That is to say, sometimes parents reach out to a child with no other motive than this: to meet the child in its capacity to receive love, and to try to enlarge that capacity by creating the kind of atmosphere and promoting the kinds of conditions that let the child grow in ever greater openness for love.

And that's how Jesus always loves. His love is not focused on something about us that serves his private self-interests, strokes his ego, or enhances his personal sense of well-being; his love is not conditioned on our giving him something in return; his love is not focused on anything he receives from us. Jesus's love for us is not a response to something we gave him, and it is not about any need he has to feel good about himself. Rather, Jesus's love is focused purely on our capacity to receive love, and on enlarging that capacity, making room in us for an ever-greater storehouse of love to share with others.

That's how Jesus serves, here on Earth, heavenly God's creative aim.

For Jesus came among us knowing this: God created us for the life of love. God created us to know, enjoy, and share life filled with love in all its many wonderful colors, sizes, shapes, and forms. However, in order to have love to *give*, we must become able to *receive* love. We were not born already filled with a fixed amount of love that will be ours to give over the course of our lifetime. If we are to have love to give to others, we need to be able to receive love. And, the greater our capacity to receive love, the greater the storehouse of love will be, that we can draw on in extending love to others.

Again: you and I were not born filled with love to give. We were, however, born with a capacity to receive love. And the greater our capacity to receive love, the greater will be the storehouse of love that becomes ours to share with others.

What Jesus was doing—and what he's doing with you and me today through his Holy Spirit—is this: reaching into our lives with very God's own instrument for widening, deepening, and thereby enlarging our capacity to receive love. That instrument is this: the utterly gracious and unconditionally compassionate, merciful, and forgiving love that eternal God eternally is. Jesus knows that nothing in and of this world widens, deepens, or otherwise enlarges our capacity to receive love the way God's love does. And that is the love that Jesus always aims our way.

In the face of, or in the midst of, other forms of love, we're always—be it consciously or unconsciously—self-protective and on our guard. Other forms of love leave us leery of possibly hidden agendas, ulterior motives, manipulative schemes, and self-aggrandizing aims on the part of those who purport to love us. Other forms of love, we learn soon enough, are unstable; they wax and wane; they can be deceptive and self-deceptive; their motives tend to be mixed. Moreover, other people don't finally know—and, so, even in the best of circumstances, their love for us can't always be truly aimed at realizing—our own true good. Other forms of love leave us, in the end, in some way or another, always at least a little leery, always with certain reservations regarding what is happening. True, other forms of love can aim at our capacity to receive love and even can enlarge that capacity in wonderful ways. Still, to the extent that they leave us in any way leery, they fall short of what the love of Jesus is up to with us.

Jesus comes to us with the graciously free and eternally unconditional love of the God who knows us perfectly, who is eternally on our side just the way we are, who has always and only our truly best interests at heart, and who is ever and only set on bringing out in us what is truly best about us. This is love that has no hidden agenda. This is love that is untainted by any selfishly ulterior motives or self-aggrandizing aims. This is love that we absolutely and to all eternity can trust not to harm or hurt or even slight us but that we, on the contrary, can trust absolutely to lead us in directions that serve our greatest good. Jesus comes to us with a love that is set purely, always, and only on redeeming us from—on saving us from—anything and everything that might ever stand in the way of our true and genuine good.

No other love can address our capacity to receive love the way the love of Jesus does. As the bringer and bearer of the graciously unconditional love that eternal God eternally is, Jesus comes to us with a love in the presence of which there is no need for defensiveness, leeriness, and reservations. He comes to us with a love in the presence of which we can feel absolutely safe and serene both about being who we are and about letting ourselves be changed by love.

Such love frees, as it were, all our soul's receptors. It frees us to receive what Jesus brings with a confidence and trust beyond anything any human love can ever inspire. Such love acts as no other love can, to enlarge our capacity for love and to open up in us a great storehouse of love to share with others. Knowing ourselves loved as God loves us—knowing ourselves perfectly loved just the way we are, by the God who knows us perfectly and deals with us only in perfectly loving ways—we find our own capacity for love mysteriously changed. We find our own capacity for love wondrously widened, deepened, enlarged in a way no other love could ever make happen. And, unexpectedly, we find the storehouse of love that we have to share with others growing magnificently wide, amazingly deep, and wondrously great.

(3)

You and I aren't Jesus. We are not the bringers and bearers of the graciously unconditional love that eternal God eternally is. As Christians, however—at any rate, as would-be Christians— we can and should be learning the experience and the work of sharing Jesus's love. We can and should be in position to see and to tend to other people's capacity to receive love, as something that takes mysterious priority over our many momentary needs and expectations. We can and should be in position to live oriented toward other people's capacity to receive love, ourselves resolutely set on enlarging their capacity to receive love by creating the kind of atmosphere and the kinds of conditions that let that happen—including promoting a societal, cultural, and institutional atmosphere and creating the kinds of societal, cultural, and institutional conditions, that let that happen.

The world around us needs Christian love far more than most people in it realize and far more than most people know how to admit. In ways it still hasn't recognized, our world is desperate for Christian love. Deprived of such love, our world—the world we're going to bequeath to those who come after us—can only become a ruinous place.

You and I, we Christians, need to face up to the fact that the world is in crisis and that we have been turned into first responders. It now is up to us to reach out to the world in its unrecognized need and desperation, with the same mind as Jesus, the same love as Jesus. It is up to us to learn and practice love that is oriented simply to other people's capacity to receive it, and that strives without hidden agendas, ulterior motives, manipulative schemes, or self-aggrandizing aims, to enlarge people's capacity to receive it, by creating the kind of atmosphere and promoting the kinds of conditions that let that happen.

Let them learn that we are Christians by just that love. Amen.

(22)

Romans 13:8–10   ...as you love yourself.

August 23, 2020, 12th Sunday after Pentecost

Greeting
The grace of the Lord Jesus Christ be with you all!

We are gathered here in God's sanctuary in this Sabbath time. And we are gathered here knowing that politics is all around us all the time.

I fully agree with the German theologian, Helmut Gollwitzer, who put it this way: "It is an indispensable part of the task of the disciple [of Jesus] in this world that he should accompany political events attentively, prayerfully, sharing in reflection and in consultation, now and then giving his judgment and taking sides." Indeed, while we may or may not be comfortable with the fact, we can't avoid being always "already involved in politics, and therefore we must go into politics; we have not the choice of taking part in politics or not, but only of *how* to take part, with what motives, with what aims and methods, on which side."[17] Again: politics is all around us all the time.

In the United States right now a special season of politics is all around us—the one that arrives about this time every four years, bringing a presidential election into every nook and

---

[17] Helmut Gollwitzer, *An Introduction to Protestant Theology,* trans. David Cairns (Philadelphia: Westminster Press, 1982), 190–191.

cranny of our life. And that at a time this year when a number of political issues have reached a boiling point and are spilling over into mass protests in the public square and in the streets—protests aimed at alerting us to and at calling us to take action regarding how deviously the likes of systemic racism, structural poverty, and institutional violence are able to shape and contort how we think, feel, and live. And all that, smack in the middle of a society fiercely divided over how to address the COVID-19 crisis that still has the power to wreak havoc on our health-care system, on our livelihoods, incomes, and ability to pay our bills, and on our emotional well-being.

As Gollwitzer, mindful of the story of the jealously murderous Cain and his brother Abel in Genesis 4, puts it, "This world is *Cain's world*. We are Cain…But it is the world of Cain which—rather than perishing from its Cain nature—is to be saved, transformed, and, with a view to this salvation, *maintained*." This is part of the divine work in which we Christians share: "the preservation of the old world with a view to its salvation."[18]

When we gather as followers of Jesus to worship God, we don't do so to serve narrow interests of our own. Nor are we to let the world around us set our agenda. We're not here to do the bidding of any particular political party. We're not here to cater to or support any particular government or nation. We're not here as the voice or as an arm of some other organization's cause or program. Rather, we are here to draw guidance and direction from the gospel of Jesus Christ so that we might humbly yet also boldly strive together to make this world more like the world God's graciously redeeming love intends.

---

[18] Ibid., 183.

It belongs to my prayer that this service of worship shall serve that end. Amen.

++++++++++++++++++++++++++++++++++++

Announcements

For the time being, our congregation still is streaming our worship services online only. We've not yet opened our doors to in-person gatherings. We intend to return to in-person worship when, with an eye to the age and underlying health conditions of so many of our members, that seems wise. I expect that, when we do open up, many of our members will still feel it unwise to join us here, due to concerns having to do with age and/or underlying health conditions. So even when in-person worship begins again, we will continue streaming services for those still staying home.

Today, there are again four of us here in the sanctuary: David Harper is operating our audio/video equipment; Sally Todd is playing the piano; Charles Gray is serving as liturgist; and I'm Ruskin Falls, here to do the preaching. All four of us hope that this service, even at this electronic distance, serves to lift you into the true spirit of worship.

++++++++++++++++++++++++++++++++++++

Romans 13:8–10 *... as you love yourself.*

TEXT *(English translation: NRSV)*

Owe no one anything, except to love one another; for the one who loves another has fulfilled the law. The commandments, "You shall not commit adultery; You shall not murder; You shall not steal; You shall not covet"; and any other commandment, are summed up in this word, "Love your neighbor as yourself." Love does no wrong to a neighbor; therefore, love is the fulfilling of the law.

(1)

"Love your neighbor as yourself" is not one of the Ten Commandments. Over time, however, it came to be regarded as a command that takes us to the heart of the meaning of the Ten Commandments. In Matthew 22, Mark 12, and Luke 10, Jesus identifies "Love your neighbor as yourself" as part of what he calls "the greatest commandment in the law"—the law that he came not to destroy but to fulfill (Matthew 5:17–20). And, as we just now read, Paul is one with Jesus in insisting that "Love your neighbor as yourself" takes us to the heart of the Ten Commandments.

(2)

Note well: there is *one* commandment here, not two. The commandment is not: "Love *yourself*" and "Love *others* the same way." Nowhere in the Bible is it commanded—at any rate, nowhere do I hear commanded—"Love yourself." Still, this commandment sometimes is regarded in that way. Many people want to hear "Love yourself" commanded here. And I think I know one reason why that is so. And I take that reason seriously. It has to do with the way the church historically has interpreted biblical references to the godliness of self-denial and the ungodliness of self-love.

Particularly under the influence of Protestant notions of the nature, pervasiveness, and power of sin, the church often has been heard identifying self-love solely with the elevating of one's own well-being over the well-being of others, and the church often has been heard identifying self-denial solely with the elevating of the well-being of others over one's own well-being.

I am convinced that there is deep truth in the Protestant understanding of the nature, pervasiveness, and power of sin's influence over us. I even am convinced that terms such as self-love and self-assertion can be helpful in alerting us to ways in which we do get entangled in demonic forces that put us at odds with God. That said, however, I hasten to add the following: A superficial understanding of the biblical meaning of self-denial and self-renunciation can and often has resulted in our neglecting this crucial biblical insight: what God actually desires for us is not that we live without happiness, satisfaction, and well-being, but, rather, that we thrive and flourish precisely as selves created by God to participate in the goodness of God's creation and to *know, enjoy, and share* God's love. A superficial understanding of the biblical meaning of self-denial or self-renunciation can and often has resulted in Christians neglecting the following fact: Sometimes, what some people actually need—indeed, what all of us at one time or another actually need—and what God, in such times, actually intends for us is not a directive to sacrifice our own well-being but, rather, courage and encouragement in asserting ourselves *so as* to thrive and flourish as every child of God ought to thrive and flourish.

For example, consider wives being abused by their husbands; consider children who've been molested or otherwise exploited or neglected; consider persons being bullied by others; consider persons rendered destitute by poverty; consider persons whose race, or nationality, or gender, or sexual orientation, or mental or physical difficulty, has made them a target of prejudicial ridicule, scorn, unfairness, and persecution; consider soldiers who've returned from a war zone psychologically maimed by the horrors they experienced there; consider refugees left dispossessed and homeless by terrorism or other violence; consider persons in the grip of loneliness, grief, or depression—and the list goes on. What people need in the midst of circumstances such as these is not to be hammered over the head with, on the one hand, the sinfulness of self-assertion and, on the other, the godliness of self-denial and of passively accepting the trials and tribulations of their situation. Rather, what people in such circumstances as these actually need is to hear how much God loves and values their life, and what the God-intended blessings of every child of God really are, and how fitting it is actively and self-assertively to lay claim to those blessings. Surely it is God's desire, in situations such as these, that such persons as these learn to feel good about themselves, come to feel strong about themselves, experience an uplifting sense of self-esteem, and go on to assert themselves precisely as God's beloved children.

In a word, we need to be wary of falling into simply equating terms such as *self-love* and *self-assertion* with *ungodliness*, and terms such as *self-denial* or *self-abasement* with *godliness*.

Still, that doesn't make "Love your neighbor as yourself" a double-commandment. Neither Jesus nor Paul said, "Love yourself! And now love others the same way you love yourself!" Jesus said, and Paul repeated, "Love others *as* you love yourself." The divine command, "Love your neighbor as yourself," is not a command to love yourself. It's a command to take as your model for loving others, the way in which you already love yourself.

What I hear there is this: there is a form of self-love that you engage in independently of any command from God—there is a form of self-love that you engage in independently of any act of obedience to God—that precisely is *not* a matter of selfishly prioritizing and asserting your own well-being over the well-being of others. That is to say that there is a form of self-love that God has *not* commanded you to have, yet that naturally occurs in your heart with God's *approval* and that even is to serve as the model for how you are to love *others*. So, the question is this: what is this self-love that God has not commanded yet that God not only approves of, but that God wants you to take as your model for how to love also others?

(3)

I'll call it *unlearned self-love*. It's "unlearned" in that it isn't something you needed to be taught, because it came with your birth. Already as a baby, you naturally, innately, spontaneously relished and savored having come to be. From birth (and, as a baby, without thinking about it!), you prized your own being. You treasured yourself such that, simply for your own sake, having come to be, you strove to stay alive and not die. From birth, you have sensed your own being, you have sensed yourself, to be mysteriously precious, irreplaceable, and profoundly worth being concerned for, profoundly worth striving to preserve, profoundly worth tending to.

Unlearned self-love is a passionate affection for yourself and your life, simply for your own sake, just because you are. Out of an immediate awareness that being is better than not being, you naturally, innately, spontaneously desire to tend to your basic needs and preserve your being.

Unlearned self-love has no ulterior motives. It isn't due to something about yourself that attracts you or allures you or appeals to you or impresses you or pleases you. To the contrary, it is *unconditional*. It is love for yourself regardless of what you think of yourself and even if you're frustrated with yourself or mad at yourself or ashamed of yourself. Whatever you think of yourself, you go on loving yourself in this sense: You have a natural, innate, spontaneous impulse to be concerned for yourself, to tend to your needs, to protect and preserve your life, and to desire your own good—simply because you *are*.

The theologian Paul Ramsey put it this way: "Unsubdued by bad qualities, not elicited by good ones, self-love does not wait on worth."[19] You don't first measure your worth and then decide whether or not to love yourself. You don't first measure your worth and then decide whether or not to be concerned for yourself and tend to your needs and protect and preserve your life and desire your own good. You just do all that, naturally, innately, spontaneously. You just do all that, without conditions or question. You just do all that, just because you are, just because your deep desire is to go on being. Even were you to ponder killing yourself, it wouldn't be because you stopped loving yourself and passionately desiring your own good. It would be because you believed yourself too painfully and hopelessly cut off from the ability to tend to those needs and seek that good. Even suicide wouldn't mean you didn't love yourself in the way of

---

[19] Paul Ramsey, *Basic Christian Ethics* (Chicago: The University of Chicago Press, 1950), 100.

unlearned self-love. Rather it would mean that, oh-so tragically, you needed loving shoulders to lean on that you failed to find, or couldn't see, or didn't trust. Unlearned *self*-love, however, is always there—and it's there with God's blessing.

(4)

So, what the Bible gives us to hear as belonging to God's greatest commandment, what the Bible gives us to hear as the summary of all God's commandments, is this: you are to let unlearned self-love be the model for how you are to love others. You are to love others as you love yourself with unlearned self-love. So: what does it mean to love others in that way?

For starters, it means loving them for their own sake. It means loving them not because something about them is attractive or appealing or impressive or pleasing to you but just because they are there. It means loving them without ulterior motives. It means loving them not because of something you get from loving them and not in order to get something from them, but simply for their own sake, just because they are there.

It means loving them without first measuring their worth, without first sizing them up to decide whether or not they are worthy of your love. It means loving them no matter how much of a saint or how much of a sinner they are; no matter if they're kind or if they're vile; no matter whether coarse or refined; no matter whether they're a lot like you or hardly like you at all. You love them just because they are there and therefore are worth being concerned for, are worth tending to and providing for, are worth your desire for their good.

And it means loving them regardless of how they make you feel. It doesn't matter what kind of feelings they evoke in you.

It doesn't matter whether they make you feel elated or sad, mad
or glad, amused or outraged, indignant or proud. You love them
not because of how they make you feel, but because, regardless
of how you feel about them, you sense them to be mysteriously
worth being concerned for, being tended to, and being provided
with what is good.

Loving others as you love yourself means loving them
unconditionally. For that is how you love yourself—
unconditionally. As Ramsey noted, "You naturally love yourself
for your own sake. You wish your own good, and you do so even
when you may have a certain distaste for the kind of person you
are. Liking yourself or thinking yourself very nice, or not, has
fundamentally nothing to do with the matter."[20] Whatever you
think about others, whatever they are like, and however they
treat you or otherwise make you feel, you are to love them in
the sense of being concerned for them, desiring their good, and
striving to tend to their needs and protect and preserve their
life, simply for their own sake, simply because they are there.

(5)

I know that doesn't sound realistic. It is, however, God's
command. I know, too, it isn't something we're going to do
naturally, innately, or spontaneously. Loving others as we love
ourselves cuts powerfully against the grain of how we, on our
own, apart from God's command, would relate to others. While
God does not need to command us to love ourselves, we are
not going to love others in this way on our own, but only, if
at all and to any degree, in response to God's command. But

---

[20] Ibid.

why would God command so—dare we say!—foolish a thing as loving others as you love yourself? Let's begin with why God commands at all.

God commands because that's how otherworldly God has chosen to give us guidance and direction in this world. God has chosen not to be a coercive presence in the world, lording it over us and forcing us into doing God's bidding like marionettes. God instead has chosen to be with us through God's word. God has chosen to give us guidance and direction by speaking to our hearts and minds. God has chosen not to manipulate us but to command us, and to give us time and space to respond to God through decisions and actions of our own.

God commands also because humanity has proven disinclined to care for the Earth and for each other in keeping with God's creative aim. We humans have proven ourselves prone to sin. We are utterly inclined to turn from God and, as a result, to turn this world into a place of sorrow and suffering, prejudice and ill-will, resentment and lies, injustice and violence—even into a wasteland. The world might not be what you and I right now might think of as a wasteland. God, however, in the light of God's good aims and purposes, sees in our world a tragic wasteland of waywardness. And across the awful distance sin has put between our wills and God's will—in the face of our disinclination to give the Earth and each other the care God knows is needed—God's guidance and direction, God's word, reaches us as God's command to exchange our ways for God's. It reaches us as God's command to us not to stay entangled in what the world would have us think and do, but, instead, to let ourselves be transformed by the God whose thoughts and ways are utterly other than what humanity has—what *we* have—been up to in this world thus far. God's word comes at us now as God's command to change our ways, God's command to follow not our will but God's.

God created us to be self-determining beings; and we, in our self-determination, have given God's world an ungodly turn. Still, God doesn't coerce us. God addresses us; God speaks to us God's word. And that word comes to us as God's command to do particular things that God knows rightly serve the future that God's love is calling into being—particular things that God knows will prepare the world for what Jesus called God's coming kingdom.

And, as Jesus said, God's greatest commandment includes this: "Love your neighbor as yourself." And, as the apostle Paul, following Jesus, said: All of God's commandments are summed up in this word, "Love your neighbor as yourself." Amen.

(23)

Revelation 1:9–2:7   Love letters from Jesus.

August 30, 2020, 13th Sunday after Pentecost

Greeting
The grace of the Lord Jesus Christ be with you all!

Divine worship is about learning to feel God's passionate love for the world. It's about learning to think, not merely from a center in ourselves, but from a center that is in God. It's about learning to do God's goodness justice in this world.

It belongs to my prayer today that, through this time of worship, we all may learn more profoundly to sense and become better readied to carry out the tasks that God has entrusted to us for the sake of the future that God is calling into being. It belongs to my prayer that this service of worship may be a constant prayer to God for strength and courage in all that we do as the covenant community of the Holy Spirit of Jesus Christ our Lord. Amen.

+ +

Announcements
I'm Ruskin Falls. I serve as minister here at Pulaski Heights Presbyterian, and I'll be doing the preaching today. Joining me in the sanctuary are our music director, Sally Todd, who is at the piano; choir member Ferris Allen, who will be leading us in singing; ruling elder and seminarian LaWanda Harris, who is

our liturgist today; and our church sexton, David Harper, who is making the video.

Let me remind everyone that we send out a congregational email each week (and a hard copy goes out to those without an email address) to all who desire to receive it. It includes a few words from me, the words to the confession of sin and the affirmation of faith that we are using in this week's service, and some notes from Sally regarding the music that will be played and sung in this service. If you don't receive that email (or letter) but would like to, let us know, and we'll be glad to include you on our mailing list. Let me note also that our September/October congregational newsletter, the *Pulaski Heights Herald*, is now available on our website.

And today I'd like to repeat something I wrote in that newsletter: despite my personal inability to relish standing in front of a video camera every Friday afternoon preparing these services for the following Sunday morning, I do enjoy the fact that we have managed, in these COVID-19 times, to provide the congregation with these weekly opportunities to gather at a distance for a service of worship together. The goal that we set for ourselves in providing these worship videos was and is to try as much as possible to provide you with the opportunity to participate as much as possible in what we'd be doing, were we worshiping all together in the sanctuary right now—which, let us hope and pray, we indeed will all be doing together again, one day soon.

+ +

Revelation 1:9–2:7   *Love letters from Jesus.*

TEXT *(English translation: NRSV)*

I, John, your brother who share with you in Jesus the persecution and the kingdom and the patient endurance, was on the island called Patmos because of the word of God and the testimony of Jesus. I was in the spirit on the Lord's day, and I heard behind me a loud voice like a trumpet saying, "Write in a book what you see and send it to the seven churches, to Ephesus, to Smyrna, to Pergamum, to Thyatira, to Sardis, to Philadelphia, and to Laodicea."

Then I turned to see whose voice it was that spoke to me, and on turning I saw seven golden lampstands, and in the midst of the lampstands I saw one like the Son of Man, clothed with a long robe and with a golden sash across his chest. His head and his hair were white as white wool, white as snow; his eyes were like a flame of fire, his feet were like burnished bronze, refined as in a furnace, and his voice was like the sound of many waters. In his right hand he held seven stars, and from his mouth came a sharp, two-edged sword, and his face was like the sun shining with full force.

When I saw him, I fell at his feet as though dead. But he placed his right hand on me, saying, "Do not be afraid; I am the first and the last, and the living one. I was dead, and see, I am alive forever and ever; and I have the keys of Death and of Hades. Now write what you have seen, what is, and what is to take place after this. As for the mystery of the seven stars that you saw in my right hand, and the seven golden lampstands: the seven stars are the angels of the seven churches, and the seven lampstands are the seven churches.

"To the angel of the church in Ephesus write: These are the words of him who holds the seven stars in his right hand, who walks among the seven golden lampstands:

"I know your works, your toil and your patient endurance. I know that you cannot tolerate evildoers; you have tested those who claim to be apostles but are not, and have found them to be false. I also know that you are enduring patiently and bearing up for the sake of my name, and that you have not grown weary. But I have this against you, that you have abandoned the love you had at first. Remember then from what you have fallen; repent, and do the works you did at first. If not, I will come to you and remove your lampstand from its place, unless you repent. Yet this is to your credit: you hate the works of the Nicolaitans, which I also hate. Let anyone who has an ear listen to what the Spirit is saying to the churches. To everyone who conquers, I will give permission to eat from the tree of life that is in the paradise of God."

(1)

There is a marked difference between the first three chapters of the book of Revelation and all the rest of the book, from chapter four to the end.

In the first three chapters, John experiences a vision of Jesus in which Jesus dictates letters for John to write to seven churches on the mainland in the region near the island of Patmos. Each letter includes three things: remarks regarding the present condition of that particular church, counsel as to what church members should expect of themselves, and this admonition: "When you hear these words, use your spiritual ear, and hear what it is that the Spirit is saying to the churches!"

The rest of the book of Revelation—chapters four through twenty-two—is a different story. There, John describes a number of visions he had of heaven and Earth caught up in a great cosmic battle between the forces of light and the forces of darkness—the forces of God and the forces of Satan. There are scenes of catastrophic plagues and calamitous violence, and the scenes include an array of bizarre figures and gruesome beasts. In the final battle, light finally triumphs when Satan and Satan's minions are cast into oblivion and God replaces the old world of darkness with a world in which there is no longer any darkness, no longer any evil, no longer any suffering.

The reading of Revelation that has been popularized by the entertainment industry focuses on chapters four through twenty-two as a tale about the dark course that history is going to take as it approaches its end. What I want to suggest, however, is this: we need to read this book not as a description of history's end, but as a reminder of its beginning. It doesn't describe events to come. Rather, it reminds us of where we come from.

(2)

When we read Revelation as a book about the end, the letters to the churches that we find in chapter two can sound ominous and threatening. They sound like warnings to church members that, if they don't get their faith and teachings right, they're going to be punished by being left on the losing side of the dark war that is coming. What I'm suggesting, however, is that these actually are love letters from Jesus to his churches.

To be sure, in these letters, Jesus is measuring the spiritual condition of each church. Where there is faithfulness, he praises it, and where there is weakness or error, he urges repentance and change. In most cases he even goes on to say he will have to discipline the church if it fails to repent. Still, these are not vengeful, "Repent or burn!" declarations. Each warning is at the same time an expression of Jesus's loving concern to give good guidance to the church. Jesus invites each church, in its weakness and amidst its errors, to lean on him in his strength as God's true and faithful witness. Then, at the end of the seventh letter, he puts it this way: "It is those I love, whom I reprove and discipline in this way."

And just what is it that Jesus reproves in these churches? What is it that he tells them is wrong? Basically, there are three things, and the truth is, all three are things that can happen in any church, even today. And we can put it more strongly than that: they are three things that do go on throughout our churches. Probably every church, from time to time, has been guilty of one or more of these three faults. The three faults are *compromise*, *complacency*, and *zealotry*. Let's consider them in that order.

First off, the letters include references to Christians who embrace various teachings of the Nicolaitans, of Balaam, and of Jezebel. These are references to persons who want to be faithful Christians, yet who have compromised their discipleship through accommodation to the social, political, and economic norms of the world around them. These Christians recognize the importance of active church involvement. However, Jesus faults them for having watered down their service to God so as not to be at cross-purposes with the powers that be, or so as to avoid conflict with dominant cultural attitudes and ideologies, or in order to get ahead financially. As a result, these Christians serve God with a little less heart, a little less mind, and a little less strength than they should. While serving God through the church is important to them, they shy away from involvement in things they fear might pull them out of their social, political, and economic comfort zone.

Two of the letters mention a fault that comes in for even more criticism from Jesus than does compromise. That fault is complacency—or, as it is described in one of the letters, being neither hot nor cold, but just lukewarm. The fact is, Jesus expects Christians to be passionately concerned with the will and way of God, and passionately committed to making our world more like the world that God intends, and passionately disappointed at how short we fall of God's good aims for life on Earth, and passionately determined to let ourselves be changed by God into persons who truly do God's goodness justice. Jesus expects Christian faith to be a deeply passionate affair. Often, however, it isn't. Often, our way of honoring God is merely formal and superficial and not at all something that goes to the roots of our being. And, in the letters dictated to John by Jesus, what we hear is this: it would be better to be Christians who compromise their faith a little—it even would be better not to be Christians at all!—than to be Christians who are complacent, Christians who are lukewarm, Christians who are without a passion for the future that God is calling into being through Jesus.

The third fault that comes in for criticism in these letters is the one mentioned in the letter we just read: the letter to the church in Ephesus. The fault in Ephesus is zealotry. The Christians in Ephesus have been good at refusing to let worldly compromise water down their Christian commitment. The Ephesian Christians have been good at striving to keep their faith pure and their teachings right. They are passionate about their life in Christ. However, they have become so obsessed with purity and rightness that they have become unlovingly suspicious toward everyone they believe to be less pure or less right than they. The Ephesians, well-intended though they be, have lost the love that is the defining mark of the community of Christ. They are in danger of, as Jesus puts it, "losing their lamp"—which means they are in danger of ceasing to be a real church—because they have let zeal for pure faith and right teachings obliterate the Christian truth that matters most, namely that God is love and that we are called to love one another as God has loved us. In Ephesus, members have become zealous for their faith in a way that blinds them to the way of God's love. And Jesus lets them know that this won't do.

Those are the three fundamental faults that Jesus finds with the churches: making compromises due to unreadiness to let ourselves be drawn beyond our social, political, or economic comfort zone; complacency regarding things that we ought to be profoundly passionate about; and overzealous enthusiasm for Christian faith that lets us lose touch with the truth of Christian love. Those are the main ways in which, in the book of Revelation, Jesus says that churches fall short of God's expectations.

That said, let me point out that two of the churches to whom Jesus dictates letters don't come in for any criticism or condemnation at all. These two churches are similar in the following way: they don't have the material resources and social prominence that the other churches have. In comparison to the other churches, their finances are poor. They aren't growing, prospering, and becoming influential the way the other churches are. They have reason to be uncertain whether or not they even have the wherewithal to survive much longer as organized churches. Yet, they are in this situation, observes Jesus, precisely because they haven't compromised themselves, and because they have become good at distinguishing God's word and way from the words and ways of the world, and because God doesn't call the church to succeed on the world's terms, but on the very different terms of the gospel of Jesus. Therefore, declares Jesus, these two churches need fear nothing, for he is intimately with them and for them, both to guide them and to uphold them.

Of course, even with respect to the churches criticized, Jesus doesn't stop with words of criticism. Even the obviously critical letters include words of assurance from Jesus; his criticism is not for the sake of condemnation, but always and only so that we Christians and our churches may become what he calls "conquerors."

Conquerors are those who have overcome evil by first letting Jesus overcome the evil in them. We become conquerors by letting ourselves become disciplined by Jesus. We become conquerors by turning our weaknesses and shortcomings over to his admonishment and redirection. And, that is what Jesus wants us to use our spiritual ears to hear in the letters to the churches in the book of Revelation. Jesus wants us to hear and know that God's judgment and God's grace work together as one. Jesus judges us not to condemn us but to make us conquerors; his judgment is not a sentence to hell but an invitation to turn our weaknesses and deficiencies over to him who can bless us even in our weakness and deficiency, by turning us into a new creation. Jesus judges us not to condemn us, but to heal us and to make us conquerors. "It is," he says, "those I love, whom I reprove."

(3)

Whatever we make of the later chapters of the book of Revelation, those later chapters are a continuation of the opening love letters from Jesus to these seven churches. Whatever we make of the later chapters, we'll miss the point if we forget what is revealed about Jesus in these letters. And what is revealed includes this: he came among us as the bearer of God's love, and he declares to us that the only form of hatred that makes holy sense is hatred for things that get in the way of God's love. Likewise, he is the one who judges not to condemn but to heal—through divinely redeeming love. This Jesus, John writes a little later, in chapter seven, can be trusted to guide you to springs of the water of life.

I don't know just what the days ahead portend for the church, but I do know they confront us already with such questions as these: Just how are we to share Christ's love in the time of COVID-19, a time that cries out for us to be together, and yet that makes being together a precarious and potentially deadly affair for so many of us? And just what is to be done about the horrible financial harm that's been inflicted on millions by the measures employed to keep this virus in check? And just what is to be done to heal the emotional toll that "social distancing" measures have taken on so many individuals and families? And just what is to be done to protect ourselves and to safeguard those we come in contact with—especially those who are older and/or immunocompromised? And on top of all that, just how are we to address the massive evidence now on public display regarding why it makes sense for the nonwhite portion of the United States to experience law enforcement agencies not only as protectors of the common good but also as threatening? And just how do we explain the fact that it's taken so long and taken so many highly publicized nonwhite deaths for the white portion of our country to acknowledge this as a pressing issue? And just what are we to do about the bitterness, rancor, and ill-will that have infused themselves into the public conversation now going on in our country regarding all these things? In the light of Revelation, we can put the question also this way: Just what does it mean for us today to be conquerors in the sense intended by Jesus?

Let me close by suggesting that it means at least this: it means realizing that we need fear nothing, for Jesus is with us here—the Jesus described in Revelation 1:5 as "the faithful witness, the firstborn of the dead, and the ruler of the kings of the Earth"—and it means learning ever more truly to train our eyes and ears on Jesus, so that we, his church, might learn to live solely from his comfort and from his direction as we strive to do God's goodness justice in this world that God so loves. Amen.

CPSIA information can be obtained
at www.ICGtesting.com
Printed in the USA
LVHW040110021121
702198LV00012B/493/J